GREGYNOG

PRESENT AND PAST

i

GREGYNOG
PRESENT AND PAST

BRIAN K TAYLOR

PENNINGTON BEECH
OF
BRIGHTON

First published by Pennington Beech, 2000
5 Victoria Street, Brighton, East Sussex, BN1 3FP

Secpnd Impression 2002

Printed by ProPrint
Riverside Cottages, Old Great North Road
Stibbington, Peterborough PE8 6LR

British Library Cataloguing in Publication Data

Gregynog Present And Past
Brian K Taylor

942.9

ISBN: 0 9526775 4 7

The cover illustration is based on Brian Jones' photograph of his
Autumn painting

For
Doreen Evans who once lived at Porthmae

CONTENTS

ACKNOWLEDGEMENTS

While the responsibility for errors, omissions and other shortcomings is completely mine I should like to acknowledge welcome receipt of Gregynog historical information from the first University Warden, Dr Glyn Tegai Hughes, from Dr T M Humphreys of the Powysland Club and Honorary Editor of <u>The Montgomeryshire Collections</u> and from archaeologist Dr Chris J Arnold lately of the Aberystwyth Department of Continuing Education.

I am grateful also for ready administrative assistance from Mary Oldham and Dinah Jamieson, the Librarian and Bursar respectively of Gregynog; for the use of photographs of two of his acrylic-on-canvas paintings (part of a set on permanent display at the Hall) from Brian Jones; for aerial photographs and other assistance from the Curatorial Section of the Clwyd-Powys Archaeological Trust (CPAT) in Welshpool; for permission to reproduce an anonymous circa 1890's painting of the Hall from Tom Mulhearn, the present Director; and for a 1960's photograph from John Christopher.

From John and from my wife Doreen Evans I acknowledge in addition invaluable details of the experience of living at or near the Hall during the vital Davies Sisters' period. Other acknowledgements are listed elsewhere especially in the Footnotes and Bibliography sections.

GREGYNOG HALL
- Present and Past

There has been a Gregynog Hall on an estate 5 miles from Newtown, Montgomeryshire, Powys for over 550 years. It lies in Welsh border country where lowland begins to give way to the moors and higher land of Welsh-speaking territory in the west and where brooks endlessly drain into the Severn in the east.

Successive Halls, all facing south-east, have occupied the same general site in an increasingly wooded through-valley running from north-east to south-west from Tregynon to Bwlch-y-ffridd between hills rising to between 250 and 300 metres. Through the centuries approach roads wherever their origin seem to have ended at or near the rear of the Hall.

ILLUSTRATION I
Gregynog Hall in the late Twentieth Century
(Photograph of Brian Jones' Summer Painting)

1

At its most extensive between 1888 and 1914 the estate covered 18,000 acres and was let out to small family-run farms averaging 50 acres. In the immediate Tregynon vicinity there were only 5 farms over 200 acres, and only another 3 farms over 300 acres. By 1960 when the Hall was bequeathed to the University of Wales the estate had been reduced to some 750 acres (i).

Views of the present Hall appear in successive illustrations below but to clarify the context before considering the buildings the reader may find it useful to examine Map 1 which is reproduced from the 1985-1988 Ordnance Survey map of the Gregynog area.

MAP 1
THE GREGYNOG AREA

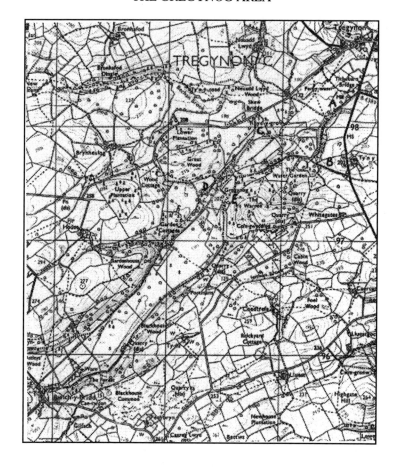

The map shows the valley stretching from Tregynon, through the Bechan Brook near Rhyd-y-gro to the Gregynog site between the Great Wood hill to the north-west and the Warren hill to the south-east and then on along the Wern Bottom between the upper Plantation and Gardenhouse Wood hills to the west and the Blackhouse hill to the east to the village of Bwlch-y-ffridd.

Several gentle strolls and walks of varying length have been signposted for the visitor from near the car-park through the Dell and past the Middle Lodge to the Duck Pond or Water Garden and thence through the trees and later across the Bwlch-y-ffridd drive and along the Ladies' Walk beside the Sunken Garden and back to the Main Building near the Bowling Green. From this point walkers may continue up the southerly mound steps to a viaduct bridge and on around Upper Plantation and Gardenhouse Wood slopes above the Dingle, returning via the ruined Bothy and Walled Garden, and Garden Cottages.

Those with more time to spare may enjoy the anti-clockwise circuit (with one or two stiles to negotiate) around the Wern Bottom starting at the front of the Main Building and taking the road which passes Garden Cottages. This is followed from the Bothy as a service track to the Bwlch-y-ffridd road and village where one turns left onto the return Wern track. Soon afterwards one passes what used to be an entrance lodge known as Bwlch-y-ffridd lodge. The track when it nears the Hall becomes a road which eventually leads back to the car-park area.

The Map also indicates the main motorable roads today. These include the Front Drive (overprinted A on the map) from the first Tregynon cross-roads (as one travels from Newtown via Bettws Cedewain, the Galloping Drive (overprinted B) from the turning near Tyn-y-Bryn (as one travels from Newtown via Highgate) which joins the Front Drive just before the Duck Pond; and the gated Back Drive (overprinted C) from the Tregynon-South-West-exit-road turning, soon after crossing Skew Bridge. There are 'Lodge' buildings at the entrances to the A and B drives, namely the Sawmill Lodge on the Front Drive, and the Galloping Drive Lodge on that drive. Closer to the Hall on the Front Drive is a more imposing Middle Lodge.

Other tarmac service roads include the Rear or Gardens Drive past the Warden's or Director's house and Garden Cottages to the Bothy (overprinted D); and the 'closed' Bwlch-y-ffridd 'Drive' which turns off the Front Drive near the Dell and continues in a maintained condition as far as the Sunken Garden Bridge and 'Hand' sculpture in front of the Hall (overprinted E). Thereafter this Drive, as we have noted, becomes more of a service track along the eastern side of the Wern as far as the village and what was once the Bwlch-y-ffridd lodge.

THE BUILDINGS

ILLUSTRATION II
The Main Building Today

The Hall today as a complex of buildings is best introduced with a round of vistas. Viewed firstly from the front, say from the Sunken Garden bridge to the south-east, the main building is 4-storeyed and 5-winged with 5 gabled dormer windows, 7 windows on the third and second floors and 6 windows on the ground floor. The brick house which has been encased in concrete and painted as black and white timbering with profuse additional decorations has been extended to the right via a plain two-storey corridor to a lower one-storey black-and-white real-timbered Music Room with 3 large semi-dormer windows. Further to the right one might be able to glimpse, on a lower site-level, a quite separate part one-storey, part two-storey, Office-and-Courtyard outbuilding.

Before moving from the front of the hall it is useful to identify the 5 wings from left to right as Wings 1 to 5 respectively and to note that the centre section constitutes an E-front with the porch-doorwayed Wing 3 set back about 15 feet as the centre of the 'E'. Side gables on Wings 2 and 4 face inwards to this central entrance. The frontages of Wings 1 and 5 are aligned, and additionally nearly aligned with the

6

Music Room frontage. From this alignment Wings 2 and 4 protrude forward by approximately 6 feet.

The decoration of the wings 'is arranged in bands, broad layers of 'close studding' [upright timbers'] chevrons [zig-zags] and diagonals alternating with thinner ones of quatrefoils [4-fold leaf-shapes] and more wilful figures'(ii). At the attic floor level and the largely obscured ground level the decoration on Wings 1, 2, 4 and 5 is identical. On the other levels a triple diagonal and diamond pattern on Wing 1 is duplicated on Wing 5. A more complex V's-on-verticals pattern on Wing 2 is duplicated on Wing 4. Lastly, the narrower central Wing 3 has a double diagonal and horizontal quatrefoil emphasis.

Illustration II above presents a late twentieth century view.

Viewed secondly, as in Illustration III, from the more distant south-western edge of the Bowling Green the side of the main building (in fact the side of Wing 1) is a 4-storey black-and-white structure with two gabled attic dormer windows, 3 windows on each of the other 3 floors and wall decorations a mix of diagonals, verticals, chevrons, quatrefoils and other styles. Protruding well back from the main building to the left is the side of a 3-storey Kitchen-and-Service wing extension apparently extended from Wing 5 of the front view. It too has two gabled attic dormer windows, 5 windows on each of the other two floors, is painted black-and-white and has a simpler mix of decorations. The photograph reproduced in Illustration III which was taken in the 1960's shows tall chimney stacks which have since been removed.

ILLUSTRATION III
1960's View from South-West

It is appropriate at this point to draw attention to an aspect of the elevation of the Kitchen-and-Service wing. The two 'ground floor' windows at the left of the extension indicate the location of the Kitchen which we will later find is represented on the ground plan of the Hall. What this photograph does not reveal, however, is that because of the obscured downward slope of the site to the left the Kitchen-and-Service wing like the adjoining Refectory and Residential Annexe wing have at their western ends, for approximately half of their extension, an additional Basement floor. That is, as will be presently illustrated, the Kitchen, Refectory, etc. as viewed from the west stand on a second floor above a basement of additional rooms. This will have a bearing on our later consideration of the nature, access to, and historical significance of Gregynog's 'Cellars'.

ILLUSTRATION IV
Aerial Rear View of Main Building
© CPAT 86-MB-1301

It is difficult to get a full and unobstructed view of all the Hall buildings from the rear, that is from the west. Illustration IV provides a distant aerial view. We will describe them from right to left, firstly the rear of the main building as viewed from the westerly edge of the Croquet Lawn which adjoins the Bowling Green; secondly the rear of the Kitchen, Refectory, Residential Annexe and Laundry extensions as seen from the office car-park; and finally part of the westerly side of the separate Office-and-Courtyard outbuildings from the rear service road.

The rear of the main hall lacks the unity and balance of the front, partly due to the obscuring effect of the extension but mainly due to the uneven and cramped positioning of the 3rd wing from the right which frames a staircase, variation in window size and distribution (the first wing on the right has no windows), unbalanced decoration and the untidy addition of a single second-floor balcony.

The rear westerly view of the Service extensions, etc. is presented in the following two illustrations. They show a central flat-roofed 3-storey (including basement floor) brick Refectory flanked by the gabled ends of, on the right, the Kitchen-and-Service extension and, on the left, the Residential Annexe extension. It will be recalled that due to the slope of the site these extensions have a higher westerly elevation than their easterly halves. The Residential Annexe

9

extension which has a bay window on each of the second and third floors adjoins for part of its length a single-storeyed Laundry building between which and the separate Office-and-Courtyard block there is a narrow passage. The side of the Annexe is of plain utilitarian design. Its further gable is aligned with the northerly gable of the Music Room. We have thus almost made a full circle of the Gregynog buildings, but not quite.

ILLUSTRATION V
Rear View of Service Extensions (A)

ILLUSTRATION VI
Rear View of Service Extensions (B)

It remains to describe the separate Office-and-Courtyard block, the main entry-point for most visitors to the Hall.(iii) This partly one-storeyed partly two-storeyed block built around a still cobbled courtyard on a site lower than that of most of the Hall is illustrated below by two photographs. The first presents an undistinguished view of the Office corner beside the Laundry and Residential Annexe and the second illustrates the more attractive seven-gabled and arched northerly approach side here viewed from the Visitors' Car-Park. As one then completes the circuit of the buildings moving again towards the front of the Hall the lower site level of the Office-and-Courtyard block becomes apparent from the clearly 'submerged' aspect of its largely one-storeyed north-easterly side.

ILLUSTRATION VII
Office-and-Courtyard Block from Office Car-Park

ILLUSTRATION VIII
Northerly Approach Arch of Office-and-Courtyard Block

11

Before outlining a brief history of the construction and development stages of this hall it may be helpful in four illustrations below to present two twentieth-century aerial views, and thereafter current plans of the Ground Floor of the main complex and lastly of the Cellars and Basements below this level. The last by its indication of the concentration of main building cellars across the 3 central wings points to the intriguing possibility (later to be discussed) of the site there of an earlier hall.

ILLUSTRATION IX
Aerial View of the Present Hall Front
© CPAT 87-MB-713

ILLUSTRATION X
Aerial View of the Present Hall Rear
© CPAT 86-MB-1300

ILLUSTRATION XI
Ground Floor Plan of Central Complex

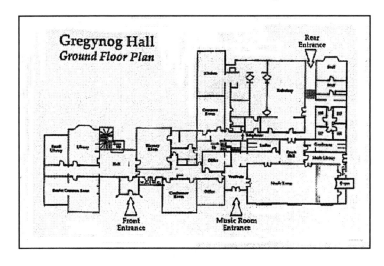

ILLUSTRATION XII
Cellars and Basements

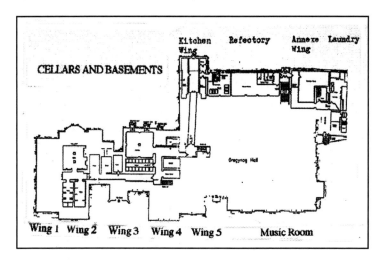

NINETEENTH CENTURY CONSTRUCTION

The late twentieth century hall we have briefly surveyed seems to be a modified and extended version of the hall built in the early 1840's by Charles Hanbury-Tracy who had become the first Lord Sudeley of Toddington, Gloucestershire in 1838. The new Tracy hall was built centrally on the foundations of a smaller Welsh Blayney Gregynog Hall which Tracy had acquired by marriage 45 years before in 1798 and which had been bequeathed to his father-in-law Lord Henry Tracy of Toddington by the last Blayney owner, the unmarried Arthur Blayney, in 1795. The Tracys then were to own the Blayney buildings and then the new Tracy buildings for a century until 1895. These owners were

1795-1797	Lord Henry Tracy of Toddington, the 8th and last Baron and Viscount of Rathcoole
1797-1798	his daughter Henrietta
1798-1858	her husband Charles Hanbury-Tracy who in 1838 became the 1st Lord Sudeley of Toddington
1858-1863	his brother Charles Hanbury-Tracy also, the 2nd Lord Sudeley
1863-1877	his eldest son Charles G H Tracy, the 3rd Lord Sudeley, and
1877-1895	his brother Charles D R H Tracy, the 4th Lord Sudeley.

Although most were largely absentee-owners - they regarded Gregynog as the 'second house to Toddington' and the 2nd Lord lived mainly in Brighton - one member of the family, the 1st Lord Sudeley's second son, Henry Hanbury Tracy who earlier had been MP for Bridgnorth (1837 to 1838) lived at Gregynog with his wife Rosamund and family from 1840 and after her death in 1865 to his death in 1889. He must, with his father, have had much to do with the design and construction of the new buildings, and with his uncle, the 2nd Lord, and his cousins, the 3rd and 4th Lords, with subsequent alterations and expansions. Land Agents or stewards who managed the Tracy and Sudeley estates included Thomas Colley (who founded the Tregynon Methodist Chapel (1798) until 1812,

Dyer (1812-1838), Baker (1828-1842) and W Scott Owen (until the 1890's or early 1900's).

Some idea of his establishment is given by the Census record on Census night 1871. Residents then included Tracy as widower head, his daughters Rose and Henrietta, a housekeeper, ladies maid, butler, two footmen, cook, four maids, laundrymaid, coachman and gamekeeper with as outside staff, three in the 'Garden House' and four in three 'Wern cottages'. On Census night 1891, two years after Tracy's death, only three 'servants' occupied Gregynog Hall.

Surprisingly little is confidently known about the nineteenth-century history of the design, construction and subsequent modifications and extensions of the 1840's Tracy Hall.(iv) It seems likely that the centre of the new building which was eventually to have a 5-winged frontage was begun by the 1st Lord Sudeley and his resident son Henry in the early 1840's on the site of the centre of a smaller H-plan 2-winged seventeenth-century Blayney building. It may be that the positions of presentday wings 2 and 4 approximate those of the less protruding two front wings of the earlier hall. In the 1840's building process the panelling of a 1636 'carved parlour' which had possibly been located in the South-East wing 'Drawing Room' of the old house (now a section of a larger Senior Common Room) was relocated in the rear right centre 'Dining Room' (now called the Blayney Room) of the new house.

The general plan of the centre of the old hall (and apparently its width to the rear) was more or less maintained in the successor but rooms were enlarged and given more height. It has been said that a new wing (possibly the present Wing 1) was built and a new floor added. The emergence of a larger 3-storeyed brick building with a further attic storey had begun. Below, in the centre of the new building, as future archaeological research may reveal, traces of its seventeenth-century forerunner might remain.(v)

The main approach roads to Gregynog at this time according to the 1836 Ordnance Survey map included those from Tregynon via Skew Bridge, from Newtown and Highgate via Galloping Drive or via Cefn-Gwyddfod, from Blackhouse direction via Porthman's (or Porthmae not titled) and from Bwlch-y-ffridd via the south way above the Wern. In 1850, however the Cefn-gwyddfod and Porthman's and Blackhouse approaches were discontinued.

At times which remain uncertain in the second half of the nineteenth-century - possibly between 1852 and 1892 - a further front wing (Wing 5) and, more questionably, an adjoining rear Kitchen-and-Service annexe were added, the latter probably involving the knocking-down of the earlier 'Office' outbuilding to make way for it.

According to Nicholson's Annals the new main building had an E-fronted centre by 1872. Architect W Eden Nesfield's 1877 proposal for a more 'sophisticated' facade (reprinted in The Building News of Dec 22nd 1882) is reproduced in Illustration XIII. Although it was not executed it does suggest that the still red-brick 'main-building-to-be-modified' already in 1877 had a mid-structure approximately of today's front width with (disregarding the fanciful facade proposed) 5 wings and 5 chimney-stacks, and, to the right-rear, part of the old 'Office' building. That is to say, the bulk of the new main house had been built by 1877 but the new Kitchen-and-Service extension had not yet been begun. No doubt other modifications to details of the main building were made by the 4th Lord and by resident Henry Tracy thereafter.

The Nesfield sketch also suggests that the concrete enclosure of the buildings and their black-and-white decoration - dated by some as between 1860 and 1870 - also took place after 1877, that is in the 4th Lord Sudeley's ownership period. This was part of a longer period of other cement building experimentation in and around Tregynon including Tregynon's school (1871/2), schoolhouse and cottages, cement farmhouses nearby like Fir House, and near Bettws, and at Gregynog cement bridges in 1880. It was probably around 1880 also that the Front Drive was constructed to the Tregynon cross-roads and Sawmill Lodge, and the half-timbered Middle and Bwlch-y-ffridd Lodges were built. Much of the large stand of trees facing the hall today may have been planted at that time.

ILLUSTRATION XIII
Nesfield's 1877 Proposal for a New Facade
(not executed)

TWENTIETH CENTURY CONSTRUCTION

Subsequent owners from 1895 and throughout the twentieth century were

1895-1914	Sir James (later Lord) Joicey, a prominent coal-owner from Northumberland
1914-1920	David Davies, MP (later the 1st Lord Davies, grandson of the industrialist from nearby Llandinam) and his company Gregynog Estates Ltd.
1920-1960	his unmarried sisters Gwendoline and Margaret, and
1960 to date	The University of Wales (with effective occupation from 1963).

Like the Tracys most of these twentieth-century owners were non-residents. The exceptions were the Davies sisters. Gaining ownership in 1920 they lived in Gregynog permanently from 1924 to their deaths, Gwendoline's in 1951 and Margaret's in 1963 although they spent much of their time each year in their London flat and on holidays abroad. The Land Agent or Manager for most of this period was T W Hughes.

It was only after 1895 at the beginning of the Joicey ownership in that year that a Billiard Room (later part of the Music Room) extension was begun and in 1903 further extended but not yet then to reach the dimensions of the Music Room of today. An amateur painting 'Gregynog Hall', Anonymous, Artisan, and undated (oil on carton card) hanging in the Library today, is said to portray the front of the main building in the early 1890's before the construction of this addition. This is reproduced in Illustration XIV below. The outbuildings almost aligning the house at right rear suggest that the Kitchen-and-Service annexe may not yet have been built by that date. If the dating of this painting is correct it is possible that the building of all or part of the extension was during Joicey's ownership.

Lord Joicey seems also to have been responsible for further alterations to the E-bow and central gables (1895), and outside the house for the terra-cotta fountains (1903) and further afield for the bothy, walled-garden and glass-house unit, the rebuilding of Cefn-gwyddfod on Warren Hill (1901/1902) and the completion of the 'new reservoir' at Gwgia (2 miles to the north-west) in 1903. His gardening contributions included the planting of rhododendrons and a yew hedge which is still impressive beside the Sunken Garden.

Later twentieth-century extensions were during the Davies sisters' ownership, and all in the early 1920's, the enlargement and conversion of Lord Joicey's Billiard room into a Music Room, the construction of a Residential Annexe wing to the rear, and the reconstruction of the Office-and-Courtyard outbuildings to cater especially for a private Press. The 1962 front of the main building with its tall chimneys still visible is indicated in Illustration XV.

ILLUST. XIV
Gregynog in
early 1890's
Painting

ILLUSTRATION XV
Gregynog in 1962

They were also responsible, notably in the 1930's for much restoration or extension or improvement of the woods including the Bank on the way to Garden Cottages and the Dingle beyond, and of the gardens including (see Map 1) the Water Garden (Pool, Lily - or Duck-Pond with boat - and summer-house) and the Dell. At the peak of this development in 1939 there were 23 gardeners, compared with the 4 gardeners at the beginning of the more spartan post-1960 University of Wales ownership.

Perhaps the most important additions in this remainder of the twentieth-century were the building of a new Refectory at the rear of the hall between the Kitchen-and-Service and New Residential Annexe wings, and a separate house for the Warden or Director. Notwithstanding the University's relatively more limited resources for Gregynog it was able to achieve an effective simplification of the upkeep of the immediate garden surrounds, an improvement of signposted paths leading to attractive views, and a more selective management of wooded areas.

So far, however, it does not seem to have had a solution for the continued abandonment and overgrowth of the Dingle and the Duck Pond or the mud-and-tangle of the area below the Ladies' Walk and above the Wern. It is conceivable that help might be sought from volunteer labour from university departments with an environmental interest and from community and youth groups who might enjoy brief, supervised, clearance and restoration projects during otherwise academic and well refectory-provisioned study weeks.

In a part of Wales which prides itself on a vision of alternative technology there might still be sense and time also to rent out the crumbling Bothy-and-Walled-Garden and the adjacent orchard to an approved organization aided by some back-up university or other sponsorship. There might be scope too for the construction of further pathways, for example firstly towards the listed Wood Cottage long-house in the west, secondly beside the Bechan Brook around to the Duck Pond, and thirdly and more ambitiously up to a new Flag Pole on Warren Hill where, who knows, above a generous new bench, and a restored view of Gregynog Hall, the Red Dragon might be raised and seen to fly.

THE EARLIER BLAYNEY HALLS
(Fifteenth to Eighteenth Centuries)

The present Hall as we have noted is a modified and extended version of the Tracy-or Sudeley-built new house of the early 1840's which replaced a seventeenth-century Welsh Blayney house bequeathed by Arthur Blayney to Lord Henry Tracy of Toddington in 1795. We pass now, after a provisional list of Blayney owners over approximately 350 years, to consider what little is known of their Halls.

The Blayneys were descendants of a lesser gentry Welsh family who lived at the farm of Llwyn Melin north of Tregynon apparently from the mists of the twelfth century. There is a reference to a nearby Gregynog of that time. The 'first Blayney', that is the first of the family to assume this surname was 'Evan Blayney of Tregynon' who was recorded as a burgess of Welshpool in 1406. One of Evan's 3 sons as 'Griffith Blayney of Gregynog' was the first Blayney to be associated with the name Gregynog although there appears to have been some earlier association of the place with a distant Llwyn Melin Farm forebear.

MAP 2
Site Centre 1774
(Emes Plan detail)

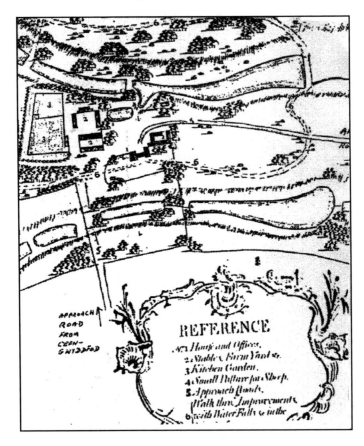

For our present purposes we will assume that the first Blayney residence was the Griffith Blayney Gregynog Hall of the fifteenth century. The owners then and thereafter were

Mid-15th century	Griffith Blayney
Late 15th century	his son Evan Lloyd Blayney
Early 16th century	his son Thomas Blayney
1550-1595	his son David Lloyd Blayney who built the 'fair new House'
1595-1601	his eldest son Lewis Blayney, a professional soldier
1601-1665	his son John Blayney (b.1591) who installed the 1636 carved parlour
1665-1691	his grandson Henry (son of Joyce who married cousin Arthur Blayney)
1691-1720	his son John Blayney
1720-1795	his unmarried son Arthur Blayney (b.1716 d. 1795).

While it may be useful to hypothesize 3 separate hall buildings over the period, namely a fifteenth-century (Griffith Blayney) original, a late sixteenth-century (David Lloyd Blayney) 'fair new house' and a new brick seventeenth-century hall which was eventually to be bequeathed to the Tracys reservations should be noted. There is as yet no evidence at all about the construction date or the nature of the first Blayney house. Indeed references to the structure of subsequent houses (although rich with bardic praises of the princely pedigrees and great family connections, and spirit, courage and distinction of their owners, the lunar beauty of wives, the golden features of sons, and the cordial wine, warmth and welcome of hearths) seem confined to the antiquity of David Blayney's sixteenth-century hall and its present possession of thick glass against the weather and much woodwork, to John Blayney's seventeenth-century carved parlour with its brave coat of arms and heraldry, and to Arthur Blayney's eighteenth-century installation of sash-windows.

The translation of the Welsh for the 'fair new house' (neuadd-dy newydd-deg) has been retranslated as 'a newly embellished hall-house' suggesting renovation rather than complete rebuilding. And there are alternative views about the dating of the construction of the last Blayney house within the seventeenth-century, some like Haslam suggesting during John Blayney's carved-parlour ownership

(1601-1665) and others like Humphreys, in view of the hall's possession of a 1670's/1680's Montgomeryshire style, prevailing also at Vaynor Park, Bodynfoel in Llanfechain and Llandrinio, preferring c. 1680, that is in the period of Henry Blayney (1665-1691).(vi)

What seems to emerge from this very slight, oblique and uneven material is that there was a Welsh hall on the same general site for at least three and a half centuries, and probably longer, that there were several rebuilds or renovations such as David Blayney's 'fair new house' in the late sixteenth century and that the seventeenth-century house was the first new brick structure in the style of other Montgomeryshire houses in the second half of the seventeenth century (built either during John Blayney's ownership up to 1665 or Henry Blayney's thereafter). We fortunately can be more confident about the site and structure of this last building (whoever built it) because of fuller documentary evidence and the existence of relevant Plan-Map, Ordnance Survey Map, drawing and paintings which we now reproduce in illustrations below. All of these relate to the time when this hall stood, most under Blayney ownership and one under a Tracy. (vii)

Map 3 is a rough Plan map entitled A Plan Of the Demesne Lands of Gregynog, the seat of Arthur Blayney, Esq. with some alterations by Wm Emes 1774. It includes a Reference key giving: 1. House and Offices, 2. Stables, farmyard etc. 3. Kitchen Garden, 4. Small Pasture for sheep, 5. Approach Roads. 6. Walk through Improvements with Water Falls in the Dingle.

I have over-printed one 5 road with the words Approach Road, the name Rhyd-y-gro for a house beside the road, and the further words Approach Road from Tregynon. Near the end of the other 5 approach road shown I have added words including Approach Road from Cefn-gwyddfod.

For our purposes the plan is valuable not for the proposals of walks, waterfalls and ponds which as many did not materialize I ignore but for the wider area context and the indication of the Blayney Hall site. It should be noted that the 1774 H-shaped hall facing roughly South-East had to its right rear (as today but not in today's position) an Office out-building with a courtyard, the complex obscured on two sides by trees. Two large stable formations lay to the South-West between a sheep pasture and kitchen garden. On the Upper Wern bottom there was what appears to be a 'Wern cottage'.

MAP 3
Emes Plan of 1774

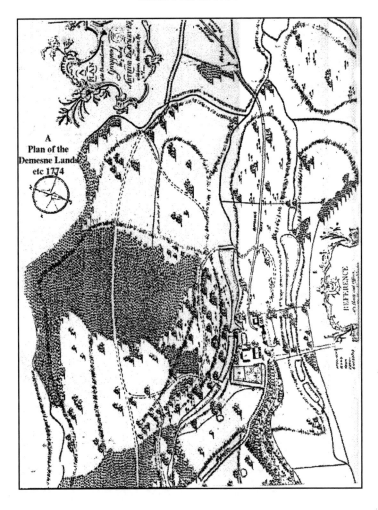

Only two approach roads are emphasized, one in the North-East from Tregynon via Rhyd-y-gro and over Bechan Brook, and the other in the South-East from Cefn-Gwyddfod. Off the map other approach roads on the East side of the Wern from Bwlch-y-ffridd and down the hill past Porthman's from Blackhouse also probably existed.

Map 4 is a reproduction of the 1836 Ordnance Survey Map in the early Tracy period when the Blayney house still stood. It shows the location firstly, of Llwyn Melyn (the old family farm), secondly of the larger farms, Neuadd Lwyd to the North of Gregynog, Tyn-y-bryn, Brithdir, Blackhouse and Red House to the East, Cefnllydan and Fir House to the South West, and Rhosgoed to the West, and thirdly 'Lake' Gwgia, also to the West. The Map reveals that additional approach roads from Tregynon over Skew Bridge and from Tyn-y-bryn down Galloping Drive had been constructed by 1836, that is the before the seventeenth-century hall was knocked down 6 or 7 years later. The positions of the East Wern track from Bwlch-y-ffridd, of that from Blackhouse via Porthman's (house dotted) and of the toll road from Newtown via Highgate past Tregynon and on towards Llanfair are shown.

MAP 4
Ordnance Survey Map of 1836

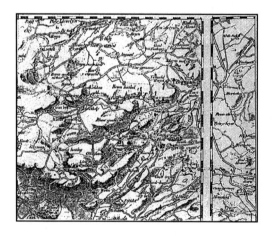

The south-easterly front of the last Blayney house probably resembled that in a rough black-and-white drawing by an unknown hand captioned Gregynog Hall 1795 (viii) (Illustration XVI below), its south-westerly rear and southerly end aspect that of a Moses Griffith watercolour captioned Gregynog House, Mr Blayney's, Montgomeryshire of circa 1775 (Illustration XVII) and its north-easterly front and northern end aspect that of John Parker's watercolour of 1827 (Illustration XVIII).

ILLUSTRATION XVI
Gregynog Hall, 1795
Looking SE to Warren Hill

ILLUSTRATION XVII
Gregynog House, c. 1775
Griffith's Rear View

ILLUSTRATION XVIII
Gregynog, 1827
Parker's NE View

Reference has been made to the views of Dr T M Humphreys who following R Haslam thinks that Gregynog in its general style may have had an affinity with that of other seventeenth-century Montgomeryshire houses like Vaynor Park together with more distant structures like Groombridge Place in Kent. (ix) Views of these two houses are provided below in Illustrations XIX and XX. These should be compared with the Drawings of Gregynog in Illustrations XVI and XXI.

Seventeenth-century Vaynor Park, originally built c. 1640 (Haslam) or 1673-1684 (Humphreys) and the Gregynog House drawn in 1795 and according to Humphreys built c. 1680 both had 2 wings and 5 central bays. Groombridge Place built c. 1660 had 2 wings of 2 bays and 4 central bays. Vaynor Park and Gregynog were among the first buildings in Montgomeryshire to use brick. As Gregynog's brick was poor it was slate-hung in the mid-eighteenth century.

ILLUSTRATION XIX
Contemporary Vaynor Park, Berriew

ILLUSTRATION XX
Contemporary Groombridge Place, Kent

The Drawing, enlarged in Illustration XXI below, suggests a two-storeyed, two-gable-winged, brick-built but blue-slate covered building with 3 central dormer windows in a blue-slated attic roof. The two-windowed wings are set forward, one-bay deep, flanking a centre with, on the ground floor, two bays on either side of a pedimented doorway, and on the second floor 5 bays. The left of the house had a protruding chimneyed end. To the right rear there seems to be an almost adjoining outbuilding.

ILLUSTRATION XXI

Gregynog Hall 1795

The Moses Griffith water-colour suggests the rear of the same house and out-buildings against a backdrop of the Warren Hill to the south-east. The main building, now revealed to have an H-plan of wings, resembles the front except that it has 5 dormer attic windows and a less distinguished central door. The southerly end protuberance is a twin-chimneyed gabled breast with two windows, contributing to what was probably a 4-bay depth of the whole building.

Very important is the close proximity of the separate out-building complex to the left, apparently grouped around a courtyard. This water-colour read in conjuction with the arrangement of the hall buildings in the Emes Plan of 1774 (Map 3) shows without doubt that the Blayney Office, etc. out-buildings stood close to and to the north of the main-building, that is to the right rear viewed from the front of the hall and to the left foreground viewed from the back of the hall. The painting also suggests that the north-westerly side of the out-building stood on a lower site than the central building.

These sources also indicate the existence of other more distantly sited Stable, etc. out-buildings to the south-west rear of the main house. Judging by the different alignment of the major components in the two Stable units as indicated in the Emes Plan Moses Griffith must have painted the rear of the hall from a point at least 40 paces behind the right end of the more distant unit. I will presently develop this point in conjunction with other hypotheses below.

Finally, the John Parker water-colour of 1827 (from a viewpoint approximately opposite that of Moses Griffith, and with the Great Wood and Upper Plantation Hills to the right and centre back respectively) seems to depict a distant north-easterly aspect of the two-winged frontage, and also of the northerly side with a depth of 4 main windows. It further suggests that the roof and chimney end on that side might be different from the southerly end previously described. There is a hint of the presence of the northerly Office, etc. out-building behind a foliage of trees. The slopes in the centre right of the painting suggest the direction of minor water-courses entering the Bechan Brook to the right foreground. There may also be a glimpse here of a walker on the road (already only a path) from Rhyd-y-gro?

As to the interior of the last Welsh hall little has been recorded. An Inventory of 1795, that is the last year of Arthur Blayney's ownership, lists the presence (presumably in both the main house and also in the outbuildings) of a Carved dining Parlour, a small parlour, a passage to Best Hall, Best Hall, Drawing Room, China closet, and common hall or kitchen. On what has been described as two bedroom floors there were 6 bedrooms (crimson, yellow, chintz, cotton, blue and green) and 10 attic rooms. Reference is also made to 30 service rooms (presumably located in the outbuildings) including a Servants' hall, kitchen, scullery, pantry, milk-room, cheese-room, wash-house, bake-house, brew-house, bottle-room, salting room, etc. The 1795 establishment (catering in the final years perhaps for the bachelor Arthur Blayney and 'his sisters') included a butler, under-butler, housekeeper, cook, under-cook and chamber-maid, plus 'outdoors' a gardener, groom, bailiff, under-bailiff, dairy-maid and brewer. This 1795 staff of a round dozen can be compared with that of the widower Henry Tracy's establishment in 1871 of a dozen and a half.

It may be useful at this point, before further reference to furnishings and decorations, to reflect in Illustration XXII on my own hypothesis of the relative location of the Blayney Hall and 'Office' outbuildings and the present University of Wales Hall with its Office-and-Courtyard outbuilding.

ILLUSTRATION XXII
Relative Sites of Blayney and Present Halls

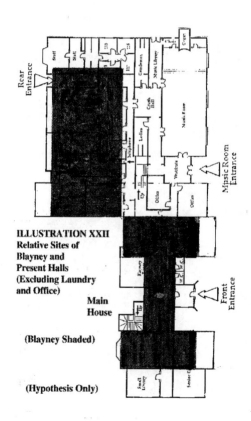

ILLUSTRATION XXII
Relative Sites of
Blayney and
Present Halls
(Excluding Laundry
and Office)

Main
House

(Blayney Shaded)

(Hypothesis Only)

In this simplified plan view the Welsh hall main building with its lower (3-storeyed) narrower (2-winged) frontage but its very similar (4-windowed) depth and its separate Office outbuilding closer to the main building (under part of the present Kitchen Wing and Refectory) is indicated in the shaded sections. This hypothesis will obviously need to be tested by future historical and archaeological research. A related hypothesis about where the painter Moses Griffith might have set up his easel for his c. 1775 water colour of Arthur Blayney's House is suggested in Illustration XXIII.

ILLUSTRATION XXIII
Where did Griffith paint his Picture?

This illustration contains various suggestions which will also need to be tested by archaeological and other investigations. Superimposed on a twentieth-century aerial photograph of the present main house, extensions and surrounds is the hypothesized viewing position (X) of the eighteenth-century painter and several of his lines of vision. These include C towards Warren Hill, D towards the now obscured side of Wing 2 (thought to be the position of the original end of the earlier main house), E towards the 'join' of the present Main House and Kitchen Annexe (thought to be the approximate position of the join between the eighteenth-century house and outbuildings) and F towards what was then open country beyond the outbuildings. For a comparison with Griffith's original overall view see Illustration XVII of his c. 1775 painting. Illustration XXIII also shows a further line of vision, that of C towards an interior side view of B, one of the two (no longer existing) Farmyard and Stable units. The other Stable unit thought to have been situated towards the south-west end of today's Bowling Green and marked as A did not appear in the painting.

Illustration XXIV (on page 34) reproduces part of a photograph taken of the hall, from roughly the same position as the painter's, in 1999. All these can be profitably compared with the other representations, including Map 1 (on page 3) showing the Warren Hill and Map 3 (on page 25) indicating the probably less accurate locations of the 1774 Emes Plan.(x)

ILLUSTRATION XXIV
1999 View Of The Hall

The precise location of specifically named rooms, apart from the Panelled Room said to stand in the 'South-East wing' (the Wing 2 of the hypothesis?) has not been recorded. It seems possible, however, from descriptions of similar houses of the period that a central entrance hall may have been flanked by sets of functionally-related rooms like a drawing-room and best hall to one side and parlours and catering-service rooms to the other.

Behind the generally plain exterior of the last Blayney building was, with the exception of the elaborate 1636 Panelled Parlour (see Illustration XXV) a homely and essentially plain interior. The Tracy inheritors found a modest mansion with some easy comfort but little decorative elegance or furnishing style. The first Lord Sudeley's son Henry Tracy who lived briefly in the old manor house from 1840 was less enamoured of its comfort and complained of its cramped and inconvenient dimensions, general neglect and infestation by rats. There were said to be no luxuries. Even the Carved Parlour had no painted carpet but simply a painted floor cloth. The Drawing Room had a carpet but scant furniture and 'no' ornaments. Bedrooms had strips of carpet at the end and to the sides of the bed. Lighting was by candles in brass candle-sticks, heating by fires and in the main house water like sanitation was probably servant-borne.

We read nothing of decorated ceilings, staircases, chimney-pieces, over-mantels, plaster-work, galleries, screens, statues or wall-hangings. There was a china closet. Again there is no mention of guns, armour, medals, trophies of the chase, clocks, fishing tackle, musical-instruments, or card-tables or game-boards like chess or backgammon. There were a few pictures including one of Powis Castle and possibly a portrait or two.

The last Blayney owner (who kept a good supply of port) is reported to have been a keen reader but there is no reference to a library. There are indications that Arthur Blayney was a generous and hospitable outdoor country squire with more interest in his estate and tenants, the village, the planting and upkeep of trees, the modernisation of gardens, and the care of well-fed horses and hounds than of household, social and aesthetic refinements. A bowling-green, croquet-lawn and billiard room had to await the owners of the nineteenth century and a music room, choir, French art collection, private press, conference rooms and tennis in the grounds those of the century which followed.

ILLUSTRATION XXV
1636 Panelling in Blayney Room
'Virtutis comes invidia'

GREGYNOG AND ITS PEOPLE
THROUGH THE YEARS

- THE BLAYNEYS AND THEIR CONTEXT

We have touched upon some of the people - lords and tenants, hall owners, residents and staff - associated with Gregynog, and it is tempting to offer cameos of a selection of them. But this is not the place. They deserve separate and more thorough and systematic treatment which must await the future labour of historians and the inspiration of creative writers. What will possibly prove necessary for a satisfactory understanding is, going beyond personalities, purposes and private lives, to set them in the wider context of the national societies, organizations and cultures of their times.

The Blayneys of Gregynog, for example, had earlier ancestral memories of the 1282 Anglo-Norman conquest of Wales, and of abortive Welsh rebellions including that of Glyndwr between 1400 and 1415. In their Gregynog period which we have taken as circa 1450 to 1795 these happenings although no doubt 'remembered' and regretted, were already well behind them. An earlier century of Norman invasions and brief periods of peripheral Norse or Viking attacks, and before that over 5 centuries of Saxon pressures and 3 centuries of Roman occupation had long disappeared in the mists of tribal time.

Of the 9 Gregynog Blayneys the first, Griffith, lived in a Marcher Lordship as a Yorkist supporter through part of the late fifteenth century Civil Wars of the Roses, the next 4 including David of 'the fair new house' through the sixteenth century of the Tudors, the next 2 including John-with-the-Carved-Parlour through the seventeenth century of the Stuarts, and the last 2 through the eighteenth century of the Hanoverians with Arthur Blayney experiencing part of the rule of all 3 Georges.

During this period the Welsh, notably from Tudor Acts of Union in 1536 and 1543, became progressively more closely incorporated and anglicized in an increasingly centralized, powerful, protestant, parliamentary and English-speaking English state whose crown was united with that of Scotland in Stuart 1603 and whose legislative union with Scotland was achieved in 1707. By this time England's 'golden Shakespearean age' (with the choral works of Henry Byrd) and the later mid-seventeenth century Civil War and Restoration were past but still resonant.

England's 'glorious revolution' of 1688-1689 and the music and songs of Henry Purcell were very recent as was Ireland's subjugation after William III's 1690 victory at the Battle of the Boyne.

Thereafter in Hanoverian times the still undemocratic parliamentary aristocracy of the eighteenth century evolved the valuable principle of common cabinet responsibility and the supremacy of the prime minister in Cabinet and Commons. By this time also (the time of the life and music of Handel and J S Bach) prompted by the growth of English commerce in cloth and negro slaves, and behind the shield of the Royal Navy, English colonialism in the Caribbean and North America had begun and among its Spanish, Portuguese, French and Dutch rivals Great Britain had achieved maritime, commercial and financial supremacy, and London was already the 'emporium of the world' with an end-of-century population of over 800,000.

The second half of this eighteenth century, the time of Haydn, Mozart and the younger Beethoven, saw the slow emergence and swift repression of popular democratic ideas and pressures associated with British reactions to the American Declaration, civil war and achievement of Independence (1776, 1778, 1783), the conditions of the new working class of the early Industrial Revolution, the establishment of the Society for the abolition of the Slave Trade (1787), the reformist tendencies of the more independent Whig party, and the French Revolution (1789). But abroad, although the 13 American colonies were irretrievably lost, British imperialism persisted: the Indian Empire was founded, Canada was conquered and gained, and the first Australian penal colony, to be speedily transformed into a free colony, was established.

Meanwhile the Welsh in a Wales dominated by English-educated and Anglophile local gentry and archaic Anglican clergy turned, in their own reformation, to a fervid if unpolitical Methodism (albeit still in the Anglican Church) or to other Baptist or Independent dissenting sects, and in their own renaissance, aided by Welsh printing-presses, publications and circulating and Sunday Schools, to a wider Welsh literacy and to a flowering of Welsh literature on largely religious, antiquarian, legendary and topographical subjects. Welsh readers will be well placed to hazard what Welsh books apart from the Bible the Blayneys read. It is intriguing also to conjecture what English literature, from Chaucer through Shakespeare to John Bunyan and Daniel Defoe they might also have enjoyed.

Early indicators of a Welsh industrial revolution to come were the first large-scale coal, copper and lead mines, slate works, copper smelters and ironworks, associated hard turnpike roads, bridges and canals linking production centres with the sea, and the growth of towns like Merthyr Tydfil, the largest then in Wales.

More rural Newtown in most of Arthur Blayney's Gregynog time remained a small market town. A map of Montgomeryshire dated 1759 shows 4 major roads radiating from Newtown, the northern via Tregynon to Llanvirinkernion (Llanfair Caereinion), the eastern to Montgomery, the county town, the southern towards Clay Hill and the western via Llandinam to Llanidloes. It has been said that in 1775 there were only two carriages in the county and that Arthur Blayney hired one on very rare occasions.(xi) In 1790 when the town had a population of under 900 there were 2 water mills and a few flannel hand-looms, hardly yet enough to warrant the title of the more mechanized, woollen manufacturing 'Leeds of Wales' of the century to come. The first through stage coach from Shrewsbury via Newtown to Aberystwyth (14 to 18 hours) was to appear 8 years later. The Montgomeryshire canal from Ellesmere still would need 6 years to reach Llanymynech and 31 years to reach Newtown. But by that time Gregynog would be in other hands.

THE TRACYS AND THEIR CONTEXT

The Tracys (and Lords Sudeley) of Toddington, Gloucestershire, who inherited Gregynog (as their second House) from Arthur Blayney in 1795 and sold it a century later to Sir (later Lord) Joicey in 1895 were English with Welsh Hanbury ironmaster connections. Of the 6 Tracy owners (all largely absentee although the first Lord

Sudeley's second son Henry Hanbury Tracy resided there from 1840 to 1889) the first two owned Gregynog for brief periods midway through the reign of George III, the third Tracy's 60-year tenure spanned the second half of that reign plus William IV's and the first 21 years of Queen Victoria's reign while the last three owned the hall through parts of the remainder of Victoria's time. This was the period not only of the music, songs or operas of Schubert, Bellini, Berlioz, Mendelssohn, Chopin, Schumann, Liszt, Verdi, Wagner, Brahms, Bizet, Dvorak and, at the close, Elgar but also of the French Revolutionary and Napoleonic wars (1793-1815), the European revolutions of 1830 and 1848, the Opium War, (1840-42), the Crimean War (1854-56), the Indian Mutiny (1857-58), the American Civil War (1861-65), the unification of Italy (1870), the federation of Germany (1871), part of the Scramble for Africa (from 1882) and the years just prior to the conquest of the Sudan (1898) and to the Boer War (1899-1902).

The British imperial and colonial expansion continued. After the 1798 Irish Rebellion was put down the enforced Union of Great Britain and Ireland was effected in 1801. British control was extended over Canada, India and Burma, and emigrant settlement increased in the United States, and colonial settlement in Canada, Australia, South Africa, New Zealand and elsewhere. Abroad British slave-trading continued until 1807 and British slave-ownership in the Empire until 1833 although various forms of 'unfree labour' were thereafter long to continue in the British Caribbean, Australia and South Africa.

At home although already a leading, capital-rich, world trader with an early lead in eighteenth-century mercantile marine, improved horse-carriage roads and canals, coal production, and agrarian and industrial techniques Britain for the first two nineteenth-century decades was still predominantly rural and agricultural with a conservative cottagey country and clerical environment as remembered by Jane Austen, William Wordsworth and George Eliot with widespread factories confined mainly to Lancashire. Thereafter especially from the 30's with nearly completed land enclosures came large farms in the countryside and steam-operated railways, large cotton textile factories, iron-works, mines, docks and shipyards in an urbanized gas-lit environment as visualized by Charles Dickens.

By the middle decades of the century with a now predominantly urban population Britain had become the still unchallenged Workshop of the World and there were signs of the emergence of a more open liberal and enquiring climate with the development of the physical, geological and (like Charles Darwin's) biological sciences. This was followed by an iron and steel and associated engineering and ship-building boom in the 70's and 80's but by 1895 (the end of the Tracy or Sudeley ownership of Gregynog, and the end of the century) Britain's economy despite its (and Rudyard Kipling's) jingoistic imperialism had been challenged and increasingly supplanted by the new world economic powers of Germany and the United States.

In Wales as elsewhere, but with significant variations as between the rural north and more urban south were familiar components of the Industrial Revolution. These included rapid population increase, agricultural advance through enclosures and the creation of bigger and more technically efficient farms; the accumulation and availability of capital; increasingly mechanized coke - and steam-powered textile and iron manufacture in large-scale urban-based mills, works and factories; the improvement of road, canal and railway networks; the use of steam-power in carriages, water transport and locomotives, and the development of harbours and docks; the associated expansion and specialization of internal and external commerce, and increased mobility of labour; the drive for free trade and easier access to world markets; and an ethos of non-conformist enterprise and innovation, and an appreciation of the need for more scientific and empirical knowledge.

In this development Wales' increasing integration into, and capital dependence upon, a wider British national, British European and British world economy was evident. There was greater out-migration of Welsh to other parts of Britain including people like Robert Owen who forsaking his native Newtown became a British captain of industry in Scotland, and greater in-migration of English ironmasters and other skilled and unskilled English, Irish and Scots especially to the coal-mining and iron-production regions in the south. Other

Welsh preferred to emigrate to the United States (1796), South Africa (1820), Brazil (1850), Tennessee (1850's), Patagonia (1865) and Australia, Canada and the States again from the 1870's. It was a time for some of wider horizons.

Within Wales there was internal, and sometimes very ambitious, migration from countryside to town. David Davies of Llandinam, for example, the grandfather of three future owners of Gregynog, took a lease in mid-century at Rhondda Fawr and later in the 1880's became the foremost coal-owner in South Wales, forming the Ocean Coal Co Ltd and building a railway linking the Rhondda valleys to a new dock in Barry. In the nineteenth century also as we shall see by reference to some of the Tracy Gregynog owners there was a similar industrial connection.

The third Tracy to own Gregynog, Charles Hanbury, the third son of a Pontypool ironmaster of Whig persuasion, acquired Gregynog and Toddington in 1798 through marriage to the daughter of Lord Tracy who had himself inherited the former estate from Arthur Blayney. In the same year he changed his name to Charles Hanbury Tracy, in which name and later from 1838 as the 1st Lord Sudeley, he owned Gregynog for 60 years until 1858. He was High Sheriff of Gloucestershire (1800-1801) and Montgomeryshire (1804-1805), in 1803 helped to raise the Montgomeryshire Legion of which he was Lieutenant-Colonel, was Whig MP for Tewkesbury (1807-1812 and 1832-1837), was Chairman of Judges of designs for the new 1835 Houses of Parliament and was Lord Lieutenant of Montgomeryshire from 1848 to his death in 1858. During this period Newtown grew in population from around 900 to over 6000, acquired its first railway from Llanidloes in 1855 and approached its zenith as a wool and flannel manufacturing centre. Tracy apart from selling properties in Shropshire to enlarge both his Toddington and Gregynog estates and to rebuild both halls involved himself closely with the public affairs and politics of Montgomeryshire, helping for example to improve turnpike roads and to extend the Montgomeryshire Canal which reached Newtown in 1821. As MP for Tewkesbury he voted for the Reform Act of 1832 and in the following Montgomeryshire Boroughs election helped to return a progressive liberal.

The remaining 3 Tracy owners were the 2nd, 3rd and 4th Lords Sudeley who owned Gregynog from 1858-1863, 1863-1877 and 1877-1895 respectively. The second Lord before he inherited the estate was Whig MP for Wallingford (1831-1832). In Wales he was Lord Lieutenant of Montgomeryshire from 1858 to his death in 1863. Little has been recorded about the 2nd Lord except that he lived most of the time in Brighton and that he and the 3rd Lord whittled away their fortunes on large personal projects of railway securities and on unremunerative improvements of the Estates. The third Lord before inheriting the estate was a Captain in the Grenadier Guards. In Montgomeryshire he was Lord Lieutenant from 1863 to his death in 1877. It was during this period that Newtown rail links were extended, to Oswestry in 1863, to Shrewsbury in 1864 and to Aberystwyth in 1867. In 1863 the 3rd Lord's brother who from 1854 had served in the Royal Navy became MP for Montgomeryshire Boroughs, a seat he would hold until his succession as 4th Lord in 1877. In 1865 he played a major role in the formation of the Cambrian Flannel Co, the largest mill in the town. In the 1870's Newtown is said to have had 18 flannel, 5 tweed and 6 shawl manufacturers. A decade later, however, this industry was to be already in decline.

It will be recalled that the main Gregynog building begun about 1840 was probably completed before 1877 and that substantial estate improvements, e.g. of cottages, farm buildings, fencing and drainage, were made by the 4th Lord thereafter. This extensive expenditure at Gregynog together with similar heavy outgoings at Toddington at a time of agricultural depression led to serious financial difficulties which despite temporary measures like hall lettings and involvement in shaky woollen, gunnery and orchard companies ended in the 4th Lord's bankruptcy. Gregynog was put up for sale and in 1895 sold to Sir James (later Lord) Joicey, a coal-owner from England's North-East. But as we shall see its years as an extensive estate were soon to be numbered.

The nineteenth-century context of the Gregynog Tracys would be incomplete if we only described it as a century of great Romantic Art, Literature and Music and of Imperialism and Industrial

Revolution. It was also a century of Radicalism, Repression and Reform.

Among influential 'Radical' movements of thought and action Democratic, Nationalist, Socialist, Evangelistic/Humanitarian and Scientific/Secular currents can be distinguished. The first, typified by Thomas Paine's The Rights of Man (1792) and The Age of Reason (1795), was targeted at monarchy, landed aristocracy and church. Associated with it were English agitations for parliamentary reform (1792-1796) and in the first half of the nineteenth century the spread of working-class protest and petition, some involving or precipitating violent action like riots, Luddite machine-breaking (1811-1813) and the 1819 Manchester 'Peterloo' meeting for political reform, and others of a more orderly kind like the working-class Chartist movement of the 1830's and 1840's with its 1838 Charter for manhood suffrage and other parliamentary change.

The second is typified by the Irish Rebellion of 1798 and the subsequent Irish Catholic Association's movement for Catholic Emancipation (1823-1829). The third includes Robert Owen's New View of Society (1813-1815) and Report to the County of Lanark (1821), his experimentation with collective or cooperative agricultural/industrial communities, his advocacy of factory reform and his and his followers' later promotion of federated unions and the utopian idea of a cooperative socialist society.

The more revolutionary socialism of Karl Marx (Manifesto, 1848, Das Kapital, 1867- etc) with its historical materialistic theory of society and its stress on the need for economic as well as political working-class organization and action was to influence the course of a milder British evolutionary socialism much later in the century. This movement had diverse components, the radical proletarian, Marxist and secularist 1881 Democratic (later Social Democratic) Federation typified by Hyndman's England for All (1881), the radical populist 1893 Independent Labour Party dominated by Keir Hardie, the 'radical utopian' and aesthetic 1884 Socialist League of William Morris (News from Nowhere, (1884) before it was taken over by anarchists, and the reformist, middle-class, intellectual, elitist 1884 Fabian Society (Fabian Essays, 1889 and the Webb's

Industrial Society, 1898, etc). In 1889 Keir Hardie and other ILP men in the Trade Union Congress helped to call a conference of 'Socialists, Trade Union and other working-class organizations' to secure an increased number of Labour members in parliament. This gave rise to the Labour Representation Committee (1900) whose later electoral successes in 1906 were to lead to the formation of the Labour Party (1906).

The fourth 'Radical' movement which was of a Church Evangelical/Humanitarian type was the middle-class cross-party, cross-denominational anti-slavery society (1787) led by William Wilberforce which worked for the abolition of the slave trade (1807) and thereafter of slavery in the British Empire (1833). And finally in this context the fifth movement was the Scientific/Secular which included the development of scientific thought, for example in Darwin's Origin of the Species (1859), Lyell's Antiquity of Man and T H Huxley's Man's Place in Nature (both in 1863), Lecky's History of Rationalism (1865) and Darwin's Descent of Man (1871). These, with a later popular and sometimes militant atheistic dissemination by Bradlaugh and Besant's The Fruits of Philosophy (1876), did much to challenge dogmatic theological creationist views of physical nature, the origin of man and the conventional basis of morality, and to substitute a more flexible empirically-based scientific and secular evolutionary ideology.

The century for long was also one of political, economic and ideological Repression by oligarchic and imperialistic rule, plutocratic domestic and foreign exploitation, and authoritarian state religion with related proselytization and cultural imperialism abroad. The political form included the suppression of the radical democratic 1798 rebellion and later opposition to the demand for home rule in Ireland, forceful and sometimes savage repression in Britain of democratic combinations and protests, and opposition to petitions for universal suffrage and other parliamentary reforms, and abroad involvement in, or condonement of, the trafficking or ownership of Negro slaves, and later the imperialist appropriation and overule of foreign territories, especially in Asia and Africa.

The economic form included the suppression or restriction of working-class economic organizations and their struggle for land (in

Ireland) or for better wages and working and living conditions generally, and overseas the continued exploitation of the land, labour and capital resources of subjected peoples. The religious form included the enforced dominance by the state church with its religious, political, economic and educational restrictions on Catholics, Protestant Dissenters and free-thinkers, and its resistance to the advance of scientific and secular ideas, and abroad its bolstering of imperial rule and capitalist advance, and its own dogmatic indoctrination of a new fundamentalism.

It was of course also a century of progress and Reform both at home and abroad, no doubt influenced by the accumulated findings of social surveyors who studied the conditions of the poor like Eden (1797), Chadwick (1838), Engels (1842-1844), Mayhew (1850's) and Booth (1880's-1890's), and boosted in mid-century by the liberal writings of J S Mill (On Liberty, 1859, The Subjection of Women, 1869, etc). Landmarks in reform included the inspection and regulation of factories, prisons and mines, some moderation of a cruel criminal code with its hundreds of offences carrying the death penalty, a series of poor law, health and housing acts, and the 1829 Catholic Emancipation Act permitting Catholics to sit in Parliament and in 1869 the disestablishment of the Protestant Church in Ireland. Additionally and crucially there were the Reform Acts of 1832, 1867 and 1884 extending the franchise to the male middle class, to urban workers and to rural workers respectively, the establishment of more democratic local government bodies and parliamentary constituencies in 1835 and 1888, the introduction of the secret ballot, the reduction of patronage and influence in civil and military service, and the reform of the judiciary. But the facts that compulsory primary education only came in 1870, that most restrictions on non-Anglicans entering, studying and holding senior posts in the universities of Oxford and Cambridge were removed as late as 1877, and that the Irish were denied Home Rule and women the franchise throughout the century are reminders of a continuing conservatism.
Abroad, significant reforms were the abolition of the British Negro Slave trade in 1807, the abolition of British slave ownership in 1833 and the granting of self-government to white-settler-dominated

colonies and Dominions like the two Canadian provinces in 1840 (with the wider Dominion in 1867), for New Zealand in 1854 (with full independence in 1947), for Australian colonies in 1855, 1856, 1859 and 1890 (with the wider Commonwealth in 1901) and for two South African colonies in 1872 and 1893 (with the wider Union in 1910). However the rampant Empire of the time which in terms of power and ideology was white, British, capitalist, imperialist, westernizing and Christian would for the majority of its non-white and non-European subject peoples long remain patronizing, racist, exploitative and undemocratic.

What of radicalism in Wales during the nineteenth-century Tracy and Joicey ownership of Gregynog ? London Welshmen like Richard Price had earlier written on the Nature of Civil Liberty and welcomed the French Revolution, and political pamphlets advocating democratic principles and demanding parliamentary reform appeared in the late 1790's. English language newspapers in both South and North Wales began publication in the next decade and a vigorous Welsh language press in Swansea from 1814 gave scope for further democratic political thought and discussion. However, most Welsh at that time, concerned about Revolutionary excesses, attacks on Christianity, and after the 1797 French landing in Pembrokeshire a Napoleonic menace, remained loyal to the British monarchy and regime.

The more educated and articulate minority were reformist rather than revolutionary. Many of the majority, influenced by the continuing apolitical Methodist revival - already from 1811 in secession from the Church and in 1816 the largest sect in Wales - were Nonconformist chapel protesters against the established Anglican Church with its English-medium worship and instruction and Anglicizing educational impact. This opposition blended with a stand against the associated Anglican and Anglophile Welsh gentry who were to dominate Welsh life throughout the century.

As in other parts of Britain during extended agrarian changes there now began isolated local opposition to enclosures of open fields and wasteland as in the riots in Caernarfonshire and Cardiganshire in 1809 and 1812 respectively. In the fast-growing mining and industrial areas of South Wales with a development of trade unions there were riots in Merthyr Tydfil in 1831 (about wages and industrial conditions) including 'Scotch Cattle' clashes between union- and non-union men and employers. This discontent together with dissatisfaction with the 1832 Reform Act and 1834 Poor Law operation gave rise to the spread of the more political but short-lived Chartist movement of the 1840's and 1850's, and also to violent small-farmer Rebecca Riots against toll-gates and workhouses beginning in Carmarthen in the South-West in 1839. In distant and isolated Montgomeryshire these ideas were abroad and Llanidloes (12 miles from Newtown) is recorded as having been the active local centre for Chartist reform agitation. Did the ripples reach Gregynog?

From the mid-1840's there began a more unified Nonconformist movement involving the older Baptist, Independent, etc dissenters and the now increasingly militant Methodists, stimulated and to an extent organized and financed by the English Liberation Society (1844) whose aim was to return Liberals who would support the Nonconformist cause of Anglican Church disestablishment (not to be achieved in Wales until 1920), and the extension of landrights and the franchise. With the passing of the 1867 Reform Act which widened the urban franchise, the Secret Ballot Act of 1872, and the 1884 Reform Act which gave the vote to tenant farmers, agricultural labourers and industrial workers, industrial borough electorates came to include a strong-working-class element who, together with a simultaneous strengthening of unionism, contributed to the 1885-1906 domination of Liberal MP's in Wales. Their presence in British politics was to bear the early fruit many Welsh desired - a Sunday Closing Act (1881), Education Act (1889), the appointment of a commission on Welsh land (1892) and a series of Welsh disestablishment bills.

From the 1880's there was something of a national renaissance with a reorganization of the national eisteddfod, the formation of a Society for the Utilization of the Welsh language (1885), the spread of a short-lived Young Wales (Cymru Fydd-Wales that is to be) movement for Home Rule (1886-) and the founding of a national university at Aberystwyth (1893). Notwithstanding the growth of interest in socialist ideas and action - a Hauliers Strike and the formation of the Independent Labour Party in 1893, the Coalfield Strike and establishment of the South Wales Mining Federation in 1898, and the emergence of the Labour Representation Committee and Keir Hardie's LRC achievement of a Merthyr seat in 1900 - the 'national' movement remained basically one of cultural Nonconformism and conciliatory Liberal Reform to the end of the nineteenth century. At Gregynog the Tracys and Joicey were Liberals but with their Anglican persuasion this political philosophy probably retained a conservative hue.

JOICEY, THE DAVIES AND THE UNIVERSITY OF WALES

Twentieth century Gregynog owners included Lord Joicey who acquired the property in 1895, David Davies MP, (who later in 1932 became the first Lord Davies) and his Company Gregynog Estates Ltd from 1914 to 1920, the Davies sisters from 1920 to 1960 (Gwendoline dying in 1951 and Margaret in 1963) and the University of Wales from 1960, with effective occupation from 1963. Joicey's tenure in that century extended through Edward VII's 1901-1910 and the first four years of George V's 1910-1936 reign. Both David Davies and his sisters' ownership lasted through part of George V's reign while the sisters' tenure extended also through Edward VIII's 1936, with Gwendoline's running on through most of George V's 1936-1952 reign, and Margaret's also through the first decade of Elizabeth II's 1952- reign. The University owned Gregynog for the balance of Elizabeth's twentieth century time.

Sir James (later Lord) Joicey who bought the estate from the 4th Lord Sudeley in 1895 was a prominent coal-owner from county Durham. He was Liberal MP for Chester-le-Street from 1885 to 1905 and continued, despite misgivings about Liberal policies, to be a generous supporter of party funds. He was a staunch opponent of women's suffrage and of the growth of socialism. During much of his Gregynog tenure he achieved a considerable extension of his northern English colliery holdings and became Vice-Chairman of the North Eastern Railway. He was a president of the Mining Association of Great Britain and for long president of the Newcastle Chamber of Commerce.

In Wales he was (up to 1909) president of the Montgomeryshire Boroughs Liberal Association and a magistrate. His other interests are suggested by his long presidency of the Northumberland Natural History Society, his enthusiasm for cricket, tennis and later shooting and golf, and his ownership of examples of Gainsborough and Turner paintings, and a 'fine collection' of water colours.

The subsequent Davies owners, David and his sisters Gwendoline and Margaret (Daisy) (b 1880, 1882 and 1884 respectively) who were English-speaking Welsh with a local Montgomeryshire and Calvinistic Methodist background were also Liberal supporters and possessors of considerable industrial and financial wealth. Losing their mother May Jones (d 1888) when they were young they grew up at Plas Dinam in nearby Llandinam with their father who died in 1898 in their teens and step-mother-aunt Elizabeth Jones. She was a strict Sabbatarian, Calvinistic Methodist and an active participant in local and wider Welsh public affairs who stayed on in Llandinam in the second Davies house, Broneirion, and continued to exercise a strong influence on her daughters until her death in 1942. At their early Plas Dinam home the children also had the companionship of a cultivated governess Miss Jane Blaker who was to remain an assertive and influential figure in the sisters' adult lives until she died in 1947. Her brother Hugh Blaker, a painter, poet, curator and dealer was later to become their art adviser and dealer from 1908.

After their boarding-schooling David went to King's College, Cambridge, and Gwendoline and Margaret had some cultural and especially musical and painting finishing education. Reference has been made to probably early twentieth century halcyon Newtown days of tennis, hunting at Joicey's Gregynog and elsewhere, and shooting lodge parties at Sarn, and the influence on Gwendoline of a high-minded maternal cousin Edward Lloyd Jones (to die at Gallipoli) who moderated her urge for fox-hunting.

Also prior to the Davies ownership of Gregynog (David's from 1914, the sisters from 1920) the sisters started their joint art collection, notably of French impressionist work, in 1908. David became at the age of 26 MP for Montgomeryshire (1906-1929) and married his first wife, Amy Penman in 1910 (d 1918) with a son and heir born in 1915, he and his sisters in 1911 founded the King

Edward VII Welsh National Memorial Association to control tuberculosis (David becoming President and another later Gregynog stalwart T Jones (TJ) (Secretary), David in 1914 financed The Welsh Outlook, a secular but moralistic monthly journal of social progress to publicize educational, social service, cooperative and housing, etc advance to be edited by TJ, and in March 1914 he bought Gregynog which was then rented out for most of the war period.

During the war years David Davies commanded the 14th Battalion of The Royal Welsh Fusiliers at home and abroad between 1914 and 1916 and the sisters who ran a canteen for troops at Troyes in France in 1916 were already discussing with another future Gregynog stalwart, Dora Herbert Jones, the possibility of turning the 'white elephant' (as Gwendoline was to call it in 1919) into a post-war community craft centre. In 1916 both David and T Jones among Lloyd George's new blood from Wales obtained government appointments in the 1916-1922 Coalition ministry, David as the Prime Minister's Parliamentary Secretary and TJ as Deputy Secretary to the Cabinet. Towards the end of the war David cooperated in the formation of the League of Free Nations Association which later merged with the League of Nations Society to form the League of Nations Union of which he was to be an executive member and a vice-president.

In 1918 TJ introduced the sisters, who had anonymously contributed to the financing of a Chair in Music at Aberystwyth and the Council of Music for Wales who needed a Director, to another future Gregynog stalwart, Oswestry-born Dr Walford Davies (then aged 49), composer, organist and choirmaster at Temple Church, London, Director of Music of the Royal Air Force and future musically enthusiastic radio-broadcaster who was thought to be a desirable candidate for both posts. This was to result in his successful move from London to Wales and his becoming like TJ with the Gregynog Press, a moving spirit in Gregynog's musical enterprise.

In 1920 David Davies sold Gregynog Hall to his sisters who did not reach a decision to make Gregynog their home and settle there until 1924. So fortified by supporters, however, they lost no time and set about immediately in 1920 to organize the centre of their dreams.

Into what was the 'white elephant' of 1919 to be transformed? The quiet, gentle, shy, temperamentally artistic and religiously devout Calvinistic Methodist sisters wanted more than a peaceful home and beautiful garden in an isolated and secluded valley, and they wanted also to repay their debts to the Wales from whom their fortune had been derived. It is unlikely that they visualized an intellectual, political or scientific power-house nor for that matter something narrowly and exclusively Welsh. They were no doubt already influenced by their stepmother's dedication to social causes (Margaret was soon to organize many welfare schemes especially for women and girls), by their own strong feeling for European culture, by T Jones' 'Welsh' Fabian outlook and enthusiasm for centres of inspiration, and by Walford Davies' promotion of art and particularly music as 'the gospel of the beauty of life' but they also acquired something of their brother's wider horizon of liberal internationalism.

The family had already revealed and would later demonstrate their support of international and Wales-wide educational, cultural and social institutions like the League of Nations, the University of Wales, the National Library of Wales, the National Museum of Wales, the University College of Aberystwyth through the endowment of chairs in Music, Geography and International Politics, the Welsh National Memorial Association for the Prevention and Treatment of tuberculosis, the National Council of Music for Wales, the Temple of Peace and Health, the Welsh National School of Medicine, and the Welsh School of Social Service. Their main Gregynog supporters too, notably (TJ) Jones in his long association with the Pilgrim Trust, his initiation of the Council for the Encouragement of Music and the Arts and the adult Coleg Harlech, and his presidency of the University College of Aberystwyth, and Walford Davies in his work as Professor of Music at Aberystwyth, as Director of the Council of Music for Wales and as President of the Rural Music School Movement displayed a similar wide commitment.

The Davies sisters' early plan to make Gregynog a Welsh craft centre soon widened and what took shape after early 1920's building alterations and extensions producing a Music Room, residential annexe and print and composing rooms for a private press was a unique and ambitious 'Welsh' cultural and conference centre whose 'glorious days' would prove to be the subsequent 20's and 30's up to the Second World War. These were the years, with the Gregynog staff at one point around 49 including 25 gardeners, when the local Newtown newspaper, after its earlier references to Mafeking celebrations (1900), the first local motor car (1902) and the first demonstration aeroplane flight (1913) would record the opening of the first silent-film cinema (1920), the arrival of telephone wires and the first wireless set (1922), the opening of the Robert Owen museum (1929), the first talkies at the Scala (1930), the arrival of electricity (1933), the Free Church Council's protest against Sunday golf (1933) and the first automatic telephone exchange (1933) but not yet the war to come, the replacement of gas street lights by electricity (1945) or the first television set (1949).

At Gregynog where the Davies were soon to own a Daimler, Humber and Packard (the last preferred by Miss Daisy for its speed) the 'Centre' now became an important base for Cultural and especially musical activities, for Meetings and Conferences, and for Gregynog's own private Press. The musical activities behind which Walford Davies (knighted in 1922 for his services to music at the Temple Church) and his staff were to be the moving spirits included firstly from 1921 to 1928 informal music-making and concerts associated with the annual meetings of the Council of Music, with a visit by the Temple Church Choir in 1929, and with events of the staff and students form Davies' Aberystwyth Music Department (from which he resigned in 1927).

Secondly, from 1929 to 1932 by which initial date a Gregynog house Choir of 28 members including the sisters and the soloist Dora Herbert Jones had been formed there were annual Easter concerts of choral music. Thirdly, from 1933 to 1938 as an outgrowth of the earlier concerts there were six, more comprehensive, Summer Festivals of Music and (mainly devotional) Poetry at which Sir Adrian Boult assumed most of the musical responsibility. On these larger and longer occasions the choir was augmented to 40 and all members of the audience were invited guests with many being provided with accommodation in the house or in local hotels.

Walford Davies was invariably present at the festivals but by this time he had additional duties elsewhere as Gresham Professor of Music and organist at St George's Chapel, Windsor. In 1934 he succeeded Elgar as Master of the King's Musick, and in 1941 he died. The music played at Gregynog had been that preferred by the very religious Davies and the sisters, mainly that of the medieval Tallis and Byrd, of eighteenth century Bach and Hayden, of nineteenth century Beethoven, Schubert, Mendelsohn and Brahms, and of 'moderns', Elgar, Holst and Vaughan Williams. There were occasional items of 'Welsh melody' but Welsh music in general was not highly esteemed.

Many of the Gregynog musical events were weekend affairs or included the weekend, when there was a Sunday morning interdenominational religious choral service and a Sunday evening concert of a religious kind often attended also by worshippers from Tregynon village's two churches. During the Depression years of 1932-1935 four 'Distressed Area Services' were also organized.
There was no more music at Gregynog over sad war years when the hall became a Red Cross convalescent home for the duration with the sisters remaining in residence, or in the immediate postwar years or indeed until 1954. During this period Mrs Edward Davies the stepmother at Llandinam died in 1942, David Davies who had married his second wife Henrietta Ferguson in 1922 and had been made a Lord in 1932 died in 1944 with his son and heir by his first wife killed in action three months later. Miss Blaker the sisters' governess-companion died in 1947, Gwendoline Davies CH died in 1951 and her old mentor T Jones CH followed in 1955. Thereafter with the assistance of Professor Ian Parrott of Aberystwyth music returned and in 1956 one-concert Festivals were restarted. The last Gregynog 'service' was held in 1962, Margaret Davies, the last of the private owners, and a tenant now in a lonelier house, died in 1963, and in line with her bequest Gregynog with about 750 acres of land and a sum of money as an endowment passed into the occupancy and ownership of the University of Wales. In November 1963 Dr Glyn Tegai Hughes, lecturer in Comparative Literary Studies at the University of Manchester, was appointed Warden and

he and Mr Percy Owen as Bursar took up their duties in April 1964. Many of the previous Davies staff stayed on to contribute a valuable continuity.

Running parallel with Gregynog's Cultural and especially Musical activities and often linked with them through those years were Meetings and Conferences, usually arranged by Gwendoline Davies, which had been facilitated by the construction of the Music Room and the Residential Annexe in the early 20's. The first were mainly music weekend meetings, study groups or schools and conferences connected with the National Council of Music and the University Colleges. Later the Welsh School of Social Service made Gregynog a home base, the League of Nations committee and voluntary groups and associations held meetings or camps, and there were Distressed Area Conferences.

A third major involvement was the setting up and direction, largely on the initiative of Thomas Jones, assisted by secretary Dora Herbert Jones, of the Gregynog Press, an organization intended to stimulate the standard of printing and book publication in Wales of books related to Wales.

Notwithstanding the initial lack of training and experience of some early printers and compositors and a rapid turn-over of staff the Press built up a reputation as one of the best private printers in the country. The high standard in physical production set by the first controller, Robert Maynard and his associates has been acknowledged. Output between 1923 and 1940 when the Davies press closed was 42 limited edition books (31 on hand-made paper and 11 less successfully on Japanese vellum) and a flow of ephemera like concert, festival and conference programmes, forms of religious service and Christmas cards. In context the books, most in the field of literature, were a miscellanea reflecting a lack of policy focus and neglect of the initial publication objective of original books related to Wales. Despite the sisters' willingness to subsidize Welsh language books only 8 of the 42 were in this category.

Reference has already been made to the commencement of the sisters' joint Art Collection, especially of French impressionists, in 1908. Gwendoline Davies stopped buying pictures in 1924 when the sisters moved into Gregynog. Margaret began collecting again in

1934. Most of their pictures and sculptures were not kept or displayed at Gregynog but gifted directly or loaned to galleries and eventually presented to the National Museum of Wales after their deaths, Gwendoline's purchases in 1951 and Margaret's in 1963. Rollo Charles has classified the works in four categories: Old Masters described as a small, haphazard collection, Early British as more comprehensive but idiosyncratic, French Impressionists as splendid, and Later British, etc. as providing an impressive conspectus of Welsh and English twentieth century painting.(xii).

Finally one should note the considerable contribution, especially of Gwendoline Davies and her gardeners headed in the 20's by Miss Clark and in the 30's by George Austin, to the improvement and upkeep of the house surrounds, the bothy kitchen gardens and the wider estate. By the heyday 30's contractors had constructed a Water Garden on the site of the old Duck Pond, from 1931 natural woodland plantings took place in the new Dingle as planned by a landscape architect Avray Tipping and later a Dell and nearby woodland garden were designed and planted by George Austin. At the outbreak of the 1939-1945 war and subsequently, no doubt influenced by the 1951 passing of Gwendoline, the presiding spirit, all was to change. The immediate surrounds of the house continued to be well maintained if on a more modest scale but staff reductions and other economies led to the abandonment of the Dingle venture, the contraction of the Dell garden and the submergence of the nearby woodland garden in heavy tree growth, the progressive reduction of upkeep of the walled kitchen garden and the deterioration of the bothy towards its present near-ruined state, and the neglect of the Water Garden/ Pond area which became increasingly choked and overgrown. Later in the century the University would attempt rescue and successfully maintained the general character and ambience of the main gardens and developed better management of the woodlands and the upkeep of some of the paths but it remained unable to solve the problems of more distant areas and structures like the Dingle, the Bothy and walled garden, and the unhappy Water Garden.

Before acquiring Gregynog in 1960 the Council of the University of Wales in 1959 proposed and received the acceptance of Margaret

Davies that the future primary use of the hall should be as a university centre for the practice and appreciation of the Fine Arts (visual, musical and dramatic) and for university and extra-university meetings, study groups, summer schools and conferences. After its effective occupation in 1963 and the installation of the first Warden Dr Tegai Hughes in 1964 (the year the 'Old Press Company' went into voluntary liquidation, and with the considerably reduced gardening staff the old house choir quickly fell away) Gregynog in its first university pamphlets was described as a 'residential conference and education centre'. These were to continue as the most emphasized functions although cultural interests were also promoted as by literary meetings, concerts and festivals (relaunched in 1988) , by the acquisition of new library stocks in Fine Art and Celtic and Arthurian studies, and by the re-opening of the Press, now known as Gwasg Gregynog, in the late 70's.

The Warden's 1988 pamphlet described the centre's primary functions as the provision of short, usually 3-day courses for '50 or so students and a dozen staff from three or more of the constituent colleges of the University of Wales.' At other times there were staff colloquia, national and international conferences, committee or annual meetings of various organizations, and study visits by individual visiting 'readers', fellows or students varying in length from a few days to four or six months. A new departure in the late 1990's was the provision of accommodation for the Institute of Rural Health, an academic research, information and training centre which was then located on part of the top floor of the main building. And so it was that Gregynog moved on, under the further wardenship or directorship of Gerallt Jones, Denis Balsom and Tom Mulhearn, no longer a country house but a university institution. After 40 years a study of its total impact, effectiveness and viability had yet to be made.

With John Donne's 'No man is an Iland, intire of it selfe; every man is a peece of the Continent, a part of the maine' in mind it is appropriate now to turn to the wider context of first the Wales, and then the World of Gregynog's twentieth century.

THE TWENTIETH CENTURY CONTEXT

The Welsh (80% of whom were already living in an industrialised South-East Wales) entered the twentieth century after long political incorporation in, association with, and cultural influence by Britain. This entailed its imperial, military and (notably from the 1884 Reform Act) democratic and later social service state, its national and global capitalist economy and substantial immigration of British and other workers into South Wales, its national political parties (and especially after 1857 the Liberal Party), its national trade-union and other pressure-group systems, its national religious (Anglican and non-conformist) organizations, its national road and railway transport systems, and its national (largely English-medium) educational, welfare, recreational and media networks (including British universities, libraries, galleries, press, sports like rugby and other entertainment organizations). This wider-than-Wales, sometimes ambivalent but often willing and positive, involvement with British systems was to continue in the twentieth century through the thick-and-thin of two great and other punishing wars, the shared economic setbacks and industrial action against common opponents, and the common experience of a national and international culture spread by the new and irresistible mass media of the cinema, radio, television and later the internet.

From the nineteenth century they brought with them of course their own Welsh Folk or people's culture and sense of ancestral and territorial identity maintained not only by the Welsh-speaking (50% in 1900) but also by the more 'cosmopolitan' English-speaking Welsh in both agricultural and industrial communities. North-western 'gwerin' and south-eastern working-class sub-cultures might be distinguishable but both were overlaid by and permeated with common ideologies firstly of Protestant religious Nonconformity generated by 'Welsh' religious organizations like Calvinistic Methodists, Baptists and Independents, secondly of Welsh Cultural Revivalism generated by language, literary, learned, educational and cultural societies, and by the Welsh-language press, and thirdly of 'Welsh' Liberal Reformism generated by the Liberal Party which was supportive of both religious aspirations for Disestablishment and Disendowment of the Church of England in Wales, temperance and sabbatarianism, and also cultural nationalist aspirations for Welsh educational, land tenure, liquor trade, etc. legislation and for more democratic government which was still generally acceptable within the framework of the British state. The viability of these different strands of Welsh culture in the face of growing metropolitan and global cultural influences would soon be dramatically tested in the new century.

The first Liberal Party majority in Wales when 18 Liberal and 14 Conservative MP's were returned was in 1867. In 1884 the Liberals gained their largest victory with 30 MP's out of the 34 of the time. Throughout the century most of the MP's or their sponsors were English or Welsh landowners and/or industrialists. Examples, as we have seen, were some of the English Tracy owners of Gregynog. Before inheriting the estate in 1877 the 4th Lord Sudeley held the Montgomeryshire Boroughs seat from 1863 to that date, and his younger brother held it from 1877 to 1887. Both campaigned successfully in 1880 for wealthy English arms-industrialist and churchman Stuart Rendel's defeat of conservative C W Wynn of the Wynstay family who had dominated the constituency since 1750. Rendel was later in 1888 to become leader of the Welsh MP's, organizer of a Welsh Parliamentary Party and promoter of the Welsh Intermediate Education Act of 1889.

Another was the Calvinistic Methodist and teetotaller Welsh David Davies of Llandinam (b. 1818. d.1890) the grandfather of three future English-speaking Gregynog owners, who was Liberal MP for Cardigan Boroughs from 1874 to 1886, and also represented Llandinam on the Montgomeryshire County Council from 1889. Although such Liberals claimed that the Liberal Party in Wales was the 'Party of Wales' their Welsh 'parliamentary party' remained an integral part of the British party and there were signs at the end of the nineteenth century that they would not be able to satisfy the emerging aspirations of either political nationalists like those in the short-lived, somewhat romantic and utopian 1886-1896 Cymru Fydd (Self-governing Wales-to-be) movement or of the more radical working-class socialists whose cause began to be upheld by the ILP, Trade Unions and others who founded the 1900 Labour Representation Committee whose candidate Keir Hardie, standing in Merthyr, became the first Labour MP in Wales the same year.

In the first coal-industry-dominant quarter of the twentieth century all three interconnected 'Welsh' ideologies began to be challenged and later in the century to be undercut and weakened by the advance of powerful new ideologies of secularism, anglicization and westernization, and socialism. These processes were facilitated by a higher and broader scientific, humanistic, historical and philosophical education and stronger 'higher' biblical criticism, by the spread of international, humanitarian and especially 'western' ideas and ideals through English as a language of global communication via Britain-wide press, radio, television and computer networks, and by the experience of increased social interaction with non-Welsh workers, unionists, students, tourists, party members, etc. in centralizing, urbanizing, educational, cultural, economic and political (especially Labour party) systems.

The interconnected impact on the prevailing ideologies was to be marked, firstly, despite a short-lived religious revival in 1904-1905 and a boost for temperance in 1908, by the steady decline in chapel and Sunday-school attendance and in sabbatarianism and temperance. Nonconformist confidence after Disestablishment by the implementation of the 1920 Act had despatched their Church of England opponent was to be shaken by the realization that both Nonconformists and Anglicans now had to come to terms with the opposition of compelling scientific ideas. Secondly, despite the ongoing productivity of Welsh literature and scholarship, the efforts of a vigorous language movement, the establishment in 1925 of Plaid Genedlaethol Cymru, a nationalist party whose prime aim then was to defend the Welsh language, the increase in Welsh-medium schools, in Welsh publishing and in Welsh radio and television provision, and the 'official' recognition of Welsh in government documents and road signs there was a decline in the percentage of Welsh-speaking from 50% in 1901 to 43% in 1911, 37% in 1931, 29% in 1951, 26% in 1961, 21% in 1971 and 19% in 1981 with an apparent stability thereafter.

Thirdly the Liberal Party, with increasingly 'irrelevant' Nonconformist, gradualist social reform and conciliatory capitalist industrial relations objectives, after maintaining its hegemony for most of the first two 'Lloyd George' decades was supplanted by the Labour Party with its more secular and confrontational trade-unionist and socialist approach. Bolstered by public recognition of successful war 'socialism' Labour was to become after 1922 the dominant party in Wales for the remainder of the century. Its ascendancy was consolidated through the inter-war depression, the second world war solidarity, the later nationalization, reconstruction and Welsh special area development, and, with the 1948 Representation of the People Act, the attainment of 'full parliamentary democracy'. It reached its Welsh zenith in 1966 winning 32 of the 36 seats. There was a reduced Labour majority in the right-wing Conservative 80's decade but it still managed to win 20 seats in 1983 and 24 of 38 seats in 1987 before a resurgence in the 1990's with 34 of 40 seats won in 1997. In that election the Liberals clung on as the party of rural North Wales and notably of Gregynog's Montgomeryshire and shared the remaining 6 seats with a still minuscule Plaid Cmyru while the Conservatives disappeared from the scene.

If the advancing new ideologies of secularism, anglicization, westernization and socialism were the main current through the days of twentieth-century Liberal Party and later Labour Party dominance in Wales, yet another, that of Welsh political 'nationalism' was to persist in a slowly strengthening undercurrent. This took successive and different forms, the first being the Welsh Liberal 1881-1898 Cymru Fydd (Wales-to-be) style of Liberal MP founder T E Ellis (b.1859 d. 1899) and associate D Lloyd George (b. 1863 d. 1945) for Welsh cultural unity and Home Rule within Britain and a related 1910-1914 one-man campaign by MP E T John for Home Rule.

The second was the S Lewis (b 1893 d. 1985) and others' Plaid Genedlaethol Cymru (National Party of Wales) stance from 1925 for Welsh Language and political Independence. Members of this initially anti-socialist and anti-World War II party were to be associated in 1950 with a Parliament for Wales campaign launched by a Welsh language pressure group Undeb Cymru Fydd (the New Wales Union) and supported by Labour MP's who brought an unsuccessful Bill for a Welsh Parliament in 1955 and a related abortive petition in 1956. Its later campaigning will be mentioned elsewhere. It gained its first parliamentary seat in 1966, a total of 3 in 1974, and 4 in 1992.

The third form of political 'nationalism' was a minority-faction Welsh Labour movement for Welsh Administrative Devolution set in an older centralist British trade unionist and socialist tradition appropriately centralist to grapple with what was perceived as a centralist British capitalist economy. After being marginal to Liberal-dominated Welsh politics before the first World War, although important industrially as with the Tonypandy, Llanelli and other strikes and riots in the 1910's the party as a whole became more 'socialist', 'democratic' and 'federal' in 1918, and was to become politically dominant in Wales from the early 1920's to the end of the century. 1918 was the year when the party adopted a new socialist constitution committed to public ownership of the means of production, distribution and exchange and (appropriate to the passing of the 1918 Representation of the People Act giving the vote to most men of 21 and women of 30) to individual party membership, and when it included Home Rule All Round in its manifesto thus putting a federalism of sorts on the agenda.
During the Depression years of the 20's and 30's (when at least by the 1928 Representation of the People (Equal Franchise) Act women of 21 gained equality with men) the party was dominant in Wales but the first and second Labour governments of 1924 and 1929 to 1931 were too brief or too weak to implement socialist or devolutionary objectives. The opportunity came towards the end of and after the second World War and the advent of a powerful third Labour government. It was then that the Welsh Administrative Devolution 'movement' began. It is usefully typified by the devolutionary efforts of Welsh-speaking Labour MPs James Griffiths (b. 1890 d. 1975) and Cledwyn Hughes, initially in Griffiths' case from 1944 and during the 1945-1951 Labour government period of nationalization and welfare state legislation

when he was Minister of National Insurance and Chairman of the party. It was in 1944 that Griffiths, building on the earlier emergence of regional economic policy as marked by the 1937 Special Areas Amendment Act, Churchill's 1942 Distribution of Industry Act providing for Development Areas, and the 1944 Welsh Council for Reconstruction Report, stressed concern about the uneven impact of centralized British capitalism and government on the particular problems of Wales and urged that Wales be treated as a unit for planning, development and 'the proper working of democracy'. Subsequent developments were given a Welsh dimension like an annual White Paper on Welsh Affairs (from 1946), the Welsh Regional Council of Labour (1947), regional Hospital and Gas Boards, and an advisory Council of Wales (1948) but for the most part the otherwise impressive and beneficial nationalization and welfare measures were to remain centralist through this administration.

After 1944 and later debate Griffiths in the next Conservative-governed decade succeeded in getting the commitment to a Welsh Office headed by a Secretary of State inserted into the Labour 1957 election manifesto but as the Conservatives won the election this was not achieved until Labour were returned in the Wilson administrations of 1964 and 1964-1970. Griffiths and Hughes were to be appointed the first and second Secretary of State for Wales respectively from 1964 to 1966 and 1966 to 1968, responsible for setting up and running the new Welsh Office with its burgeoning departments and quasi-governmental bodies.

This 'Welsh' civic apparatus was to be augmented by additional governmental and non-governmental organizations (the later including Welshified 'regional' TUC, party and media bodies) during the 1970-1974 Heath Conservative and the 1974-1979 Wilson Labour governments. It was an apparatus still largely centrally controlled from London but at the same time significantly a set of palpable civic institutions, in position in Wales, contributing to a new sense of Welsh civic (additional to historical linguistic and cultural) identity and constituting a social machinery now ripe for political 'nationalist' take-over.

Already in the 1960's in the light of Welsh proposals, including those of Cledwyn Hughes in 1966/1967 for an elected assembly and for the reorganization of local government, and of an upsurge in Scottish nationalism and the uncertain pressures of Plaid Cymru and associated militant groups, there was increasing government and party-political recognition of devolutionary and nationalist demands which the government no doubt hoped might be partly met or profitably delayed by their 1969 establishment of the Crowther (later Kilbrandon) Royal Commission on the Constitution to consider Scottish and Welsh devolution options.

When this Commission's report recommending an elected Assembly for Wales appeared in 1973 it closely followed Britain's 1972 entry into the European Economic Community and closely preceded the 1974 reorganization of Welsh local government into a reduced 8 counties and 37 districts. These changed circumstances were part of the backdrop of the later February and October Labour-winning elections, the framing of the Labour Party's devolution policy for Scotland and Wales, the passing of associated legislation, notably the 1978 Wales Act with provision for a Welsh Assembly referendum requiring 40% of the electorate in favour, and the holding of the referendum in March 1979 when the devolution policy for a Welsh Assembly without fiscal or primary legislative powers was decisively rejected by a 4 to 1 majority. Reference to the devolutionist campaigns preceding this referendum and preceding the successful 1997 referendum, 20 (including 18 Conservative government) years later (during which in 1981 Plaid Cymru described itself in support of a Welsh 'decentralist socialist state') will be noted below in our mention of the next twentieth century variant of Welsh political 'nationalism'.

The fourth form of political 'nationalism' was a minority-faction Welsh Labour-initiated but increasingly cross-party (non Conservative) movement for Welsh Political Devolution There were two major devolutionist campaigns, the first - the Wales for the Assembly Campaign - launched in the winter of 1978/1979 before the first unsuccessful 1979 Referendum, and the second - the Yes for Wales campaign - launched by Labour MP's Ron Davies and Peter Hain, and organized by Leighton Andrews and Professor Kevin

Morgan (as Chairman), in February 1997. This was before the May 1997 general election after which Ron Davies became the Secretary of State for Wales, and before the second September 1997 Referendum which voted on a low but adequate turn-out and by a small majority in favour of a Welsh Assembly. This after its election in April came into existence with 28 Labour, 17 Plaid Cymru, 9 Conservative and 6 Liberal Democrat members in May 1999. When it came it brought with it a reassertion of 'Welshness' but the old objectives of political independence or autonomy and of Welsh socialism seemed to have been abandoned.

End-of-century Welsh devolutionist literature suggests that the Welsh Assembly objective and achievement, taken together with the 1994 Act and subsequent 1996 further Local Government reorganization into 22 single tier units, were mainly conceived as a means to decentralized, democratic self-government within the protective and productive context of the still territorially-secure British nation state (which might in time become more federalist) and within the European Union (which might in time become more accessible and responsive). The Welsh Assembly, it was said, would in partnership with local government and in collaboration with business and voluntary organizations promote a more Welsh, inclusive, cooperative and 'patriotic' politics, a more open, meritocratic and 'interactive' administration, and a more popular and productive channel for the resources of Whitehall and Brussels. All this would contribute to a more democratic Wales enjoying a more innovative and balanced economic and environmental development and in due course, through research, education and training, a better informed citizenry and more confident 'civic capacity'.

Two subjects which received relatively little treatment were the implications for traditional Welsh culture (for example its viability in the face of British, European, Atlanticist and world culture) and the prospects of a more 'democratic' Welsh economy (in the face of global capitalism and what remained of Welsh socialist aspirations). Did this mean that the old ideas of Welsh cultural and collectivist economic autonomy also had been abandoned as unrealistic?

All this perhaps was contributing to a clearer view of Welsh identity. How Welsh were the Welsh, how British, how European and how global? What was the dream and what the reality?

We turn now finally from the Wales to the World of Gregynog of the Twentieth Century. The reality widens.

This was the century (in its first half) of the continued spread or consolidation of Western (European and American) and Eastern (Japanese) imperialism, of conflict between competing capitalist imperialist states in the First World War (1914-1918 with US entry in 1917), of the rise of Japan, and of the Russian and Communist revolutions in 1905 and 1907 (with Lenin's 1917-1924 promotion of a universal communist ideology). There was the emergence of the United States and the Soviet Union as superpowers leading to the eclipse of a Europe-centred political world, of Stalin's more nationalistic communism (1924-1953), of the capitalist Great Depression (1929-1933), of fascist or nationalist reaction in Mussolini's Italy (from 1922), Hitler's Germany (from 1933) and Franco's Spain (from 1936). There was the Second World War (1939-1945 with Soviet, Japanese and United States entry in 1941).

From this war, from the previous 6 great powers, there emerged among the 'victors' the two superpowers, the capitalist United States and the socialist Soviet Union remembering their respective 400,000 and over 20 million war casualties, and two great powers, capitalist Britain (initially with a Labour government) and earlier occupied France with 468,000 and 580,000 casualties, and among the defeated the two severely damaged major powers, capitalist Germany and atom-bombed Japan with empires lost and 7 million and over 2 million dead or injured. Although then in a spirit of wartime cooperation the 'Big 3' victorious nations (USA, USSR and Britain) agreed in 1945 at Yalta and Potsdam about a joint occupation (with France) of a 4-zoned Germany and the cession of Eastern Europe to the Russians their subsequent aggressive pursuit of national interests (notably of security, economic reconstruction and expansion, and promotion of conflicting economic and political ideologies) soon led to the beginning and rapid globalization and militarization of a hostile struggle later to be known as the Cold War.

66

There was partial decolonization of Mediterranean Arab lands in Syria, the Lebanon and Trans-Jordan in 1946, in Egypt in 1947 and Palestine in 1948, with the forced partition of Palestine in 1948, followed by the Jewish declaration of the state of Israel and the consequent Arab-Israeli war of 1948-1949. There was mounting restiveness in Asia against the West partially met by Britain's granting of Indian Independence in 1947 but not by the French and Dutch in the same democratic way in Indochina (Vietnam, Laos and Cambodia) and Indonesia, and there was the establishment of the Chinese People's Republic in 1949 which together with the USSR brought almost one third of the world's population within the orbit of powerful socialist states.

This was the century also (mainly in its second half) of the outbreak and relentless prosecution of the 1945-1991 Cold War between the United States - together with old and now new Western (West German) and Eastern (Japanese) capitalist allies - and the Soviet Union, with a brief arms control detente (1969-1979) and further arms race (star wars) confrontation until resumed arms control talks with Gorbachev from 1985, the Intermediate Nuclear Forces treaty of 1987 and the 'end' of the war and associated 'collapse' of the Soviet Union in 1991. In this period, and especially in the 50's and 60's, there was further dismantlement of European (British, French, Dutch, Belgian and Portuguese) political but not economic 'empires' and the emergence or re-emergence and greater assertiveness of new nations and nationalisms in the rapidly populating 'Third World'.

In the Cold War the American stance was for the global containment of Soviet and later Chinese Communism, regarded as a threat firstly to American and Western security in an atomic age, secondly to the maintenance and expansion of their capitalist national and international economic system, and thirdly to the preservation and dissemination of national and western ideologies and ways of life. The Soviet stance similarly concerned with national security, economic recovery, reconstruction and advance, and promotion of ways of life and thought was against Western Capitalism and Imperialism. To achieve these ends the main protagonists raced to build up massive conventional and nuclear and ballistic missile military forces and to engage in a range of military, economic, political, intelligence and ideological operations to gain control of resources and markets and increase their power and influence. These included intrusions in Europe, the Middle East, Africa, Asia and Latin America. In an era of decolonization and national liberation from foreign or local domination, processes favoured and promoted by the Russians, America worked in these areas to support pro-Western elements and to oppose movements for left-wing reform.

Industrialised and increasingly urbanized Britain in the first warring quarter of the twentieth century began to emerge as a broadly democratic social service state. There was an increase in government social legislation at both national and local levels during Balfour's Conservative ministry (1902-1905) through the last Liberal ministries of Campbell Bannerman (1905-1908) and Asquith (1908-1915), the Liberal Coalition ministries of Asquith (1915-1916) and Lloyd George (1916-1922), the Conservative ministries of Bonar Law (1922-1923) and Baldwin (1923-1924), and the first brief Labour ministry of Ramsay MacDonald (1924).

Ideologically there was an advance in science (especially of physics) and the spread (through education, improved mobility and mass media) of these and democratic, socialist, feminist and erotic ideas and values. In technology there was an increase in the use of machines for transportation (motor cars, lorries, trams, buses, aircraft and ships), for communication (gramophone, radio, telephone, cinema, etc), for public and domestic lighting and heating, and for domestic appliances (cookers, refrigerators, washers, irons, cleaners, etc) powered by oil-fuelled internal combustion engines or electricity.

Economically although, in the face of competition from larger and more powerful countries, her great nineteenth-century coal, iron, ship-building and cotton exporting industries began to decline and suffered severely with high unemployment in times of capitalist instability Britain remained a world leader in commerce, banking, finance, insurance and merchant shipping, and one of the most affluent countries enjoying (despite significant class and regional differences) a steadily rising standard of living. The emergence of new heavy and lighter industries produced a shift in industrial location from some of the traditional northern and Welsh centres to the south and south-east which contributed in some cases to a serious imbalance in regional development.

This was the period also of some pacifist opposition to war generally, namely Angell's The Great Illusion (1900), the Education Act (1902) which established a national system of secondary education, the setting up of the Women's Social and Political Union (1903) leading to the later militant suffragette movement (1904-1913), a seminal French Impressionist Exhibition in London (1905), H G Wells' novel of the Common Man Kipps (1905), Galsworthy's satirical novel of upper middle class life The Man of Property (1906), the establishment of the Labour Party (1906), the Old Age Pensions Act (1908), the Housing and Town Planning Act (1909), the South Africa Act (1910), the Parliament Act (1911) reducing the power of the Lords, the National Insurance Act (1911), Labour Strikes (1910-1914), a seminal Post-Impressionist exhibition in London (1910), the Welsh Disestablishment Act (1914) the third unsuccessful Irish Home Rule Bill (1912-1914) and of course the First World War (1914-1918).

It was also the period of both the Irish Easter Rising and Einstein's General Theory of Relativity in 1916, translations of the works of Dostoevsky and Freud (1912, 1913) which influenced the treatment of instinct, consciousness and sexuality in the works of D H Lawrence (Sons and Lovers 1913 and The Rainbow 1915) and James Joyce (Ulysses 1922), the Representation of the People Act (1918) which gave the vote to men over 21 and women over 30, the 1918 war-time disenchantment of poet Wilfred Owen, the Housing and Town Planning Act (1919), further Labour Strikes (1919-1921), the Home Rule Act (1919), the establishment of the League of Nations (1920), the Government of Ireland Act (1920), T S Eliot's The Wasteland (1922) with its concern about the futility of an irreligious society, the republican Civil War in Ireland (1922-1923), the Housing Act (1924) and the Widows', Orphans', and Old Age Contributory Pensions Act (1925).

In the second warring quarter of the twentieth century Britain was governed by Baldwin's second Conservative ministry (1924-1929), MacDonald's second Labour ministry (1929-1931), MacDonalds's largely Conservative National ministry (1931-1935), Baldwin's National ministry (1935-1937), Neville Chamberlain's National ministry (1937-1940), Churchill's Coalition ministry (1940-1945) and Attlee's Labour ministries (1945-1951). It was a time of further Liberal Party decline. The 1945 Labour government was the third Labour government but the first that held both office and (with its large absolute majority) effective power.

In this quarter while still slowly and expensively defending and promoting imperial interests by embarking secretly in 1946 on its own nationalistic nuclear programme and in 1949 adopting a pro-Western Union NATO stance against the Russians, the British government had become more politically democratic - at home in its 1928 extension of the franchise to all adult women, and abroad in its granting of independence to Burma in 1946, to India and Pakistan in 1947 and to Ceylon (the later Sri Lanka) in 1949, a combined population representing over two-thirds of the Commonwealth. It had become more structurally centralized in its establishment of national ministries from 1931 to 1940 and a coalition ministry from 1940 to 1945, the better to grapple with interwar economic and World War II military problems, more socialist in its wartime economic mobilization and postwar 1945-1951 economic nationalization programmes, and more socially democratic in its laying the foundations during and after the war of the future 'Welfare State'.

Ideologically there was considerable advance in the sciences of medicine, biochemistry, nuclear physics, radio-astronomy and genetics and several popularizations of philosophy, science and mathematics. These included H G Wells, J Huxley and G P Wells' The Science of Life (1929), J Jeans' The Mysterious Universe (1930), Bertrand Russell's The Scientific Outlook (1931), Power (1938) and A History of Western Philosophy (1946), and Lancelot Hogben's Mathematics for the Million (1937) and Science for the Citizen (1938).

In the ideas and activities of popular culture, broadened and in some cases standardized through use of new means of mass and centralized communication (gramophone recordings, cinema, press and advertising, public libraries, radio and agencies of sport and

70

social entertainment) and of transport (the car especially but also the aeroplane) there began to emerge something of additional 'American' secular but not American religious life patterns. These can be exemplified by the dominance of Hollywood films and the long-standing and growing influence of American jazz music and swing, bop, jive and jitterbug dance, and the widely perceived attractions of surface and aerial vehicular speed and mobility. Here perhaps were the seeds of 'faster' non-traditional, occasionally rebellious but largely hedonistic youth cultures to come.

Economically, despite continued technical progress and an uneven rise of living standards, and a brief replacement boom after the first world war and a rearmament surge before, and boom during, the second, Britain suffered a severe depression in the interwar years with a phenomenal 3 million unemployed in 1932. Recourse to protectionism and imperial or empire preference, and a swing to service and consumption industries, and later the advantageous military defeat and temporary economic prostration of major competitors Germany and Japan would not for much longer mask a trend towards lasting loss or decline of British markets.

This second quarter was the period notably of the General Strike (1926), the Trade Disputes Act (1927) declaring general or 'sympathetic' strikes (and lock-outs) illegal, the Representation of the People (Equal Franchise) Act (1928) which gave the vote to women over the age of 21 (replacing the previous 30 year entry point), the Wall Street Crash (1929) and the Great Depression (1929-1931). It included the Statute of Westminster (1931) legalizing under the British Crown the independence of the earlier self-governing white dominions of Canada, Australia, New Zealand and South Africa together with the Irish Free State (1922) who later as a republic was to reject a British head of state, Aldous Huxley's Brave New World (1932) which satirized beliefs in a well-ordered mechanical world, the short-lived left-wing poetry of Auden and others in the mid-thirties, Walford Davies succeeding Elgar as Master of the King's Musick (1934), J M Keynes' General Theory of Employment Interest and Money (1936) advocating a managed mixed economy, and the Agreement with Eire (1938) in which a

71

largely but not completely republican constitution was recognized under the British Crown.

It was the period of the Second World War (1939-1945), the Evacuation of Dunkirk (May/June 1940), the Battle of Britain (August/September 1940), the Beveridge Report (1942) on the improvement of the social services, George Orwell's Animal Farm (1943) against the centralizing state, F A Hayek's The Road to Serfdom (1944) which attacked state control and planning, the Town and Country Planning Act (1944), the Education Act (1944) establishing a compulsory state system of secondary education, Gunnar Myrdal's An American Dilemma: The Negro Problem and Modern Democracy (1944), the Distribution of Industry Act (1945), the establishment of the International Bank of Reconstruction and Development (later called the World Bank) and the International Monetary Fund-IMF (1945, both later becoming specialized UN agencies), the American atomic bombing of Hiroshima and Nagasaki (1945), the Victory Parade (1946), the National Insurance Act (1946), the National Health Service Act (1946), the reopening of the BBC television service in 1946, the Royal Wedding (1947), the 1947 European Recovery Programme (Marshall Plan for US assistance to Europe) leading to the establishment of the 1948 (Organization for European Economic Cooperation, O C Cox's Caste, Class and Race (1948) which was an exploitative economic class analysis of race relations through centuries of white imperialism, the establishment of the United Nations Organization (1949), the Russian explosion of a test atomic bomb (1949), the Council for Mutual Economic Assistance (COMECON) set up in 1949 to promote economic development in socialist bloc countries, and the establishment of the North Atlantic Treaty Organization (1949).

In the third quarter of the twentieth century Britain, after the end of Attlee's Labour ministry in 1951, was governed by Churchill's (and from 1955 Eden's) Conservative ministry (1951-1955), Eden's (and from 1957 Macmillan's) ministry (1955-1959) Macmillan's (and from 1963 Douglas Home's) ministry (1959-1964), [Macmillan's resignation coinciding with the end of the last private, namely Margaret Davies, occupation of Gregynog], Wilson's Labour ministry with an overall majority of 4 (1964-1966), Wilson's second

Labour ministry (1966-1970) and Heath's Conservative ministry (1970-1974).

In this period, its economic and military power increasingly overtaken by larger competitors, Britain over-extended itself firstly by maintaining a global anti-Communist Great Power stance in divided Europe, the Middle East, South-East Asia and elsewhere, with costly nuclear and other military programmes associated for example with NATO (1949-) the Baghdad Pact (1954-) and SEATO (1945-1975), and secondly, in its imperial role, by heavy commitments in its still unwieldy and restive 'Empire'. These latter trouble-spots included Malaya (1950-), Egypt/Sudan (1951), the Central African Federation (1953-1963), Kenya (1954), Suez (1954), Cyprus (1955-1959), Suez again (1956), the West Indies Federation (1958-1962), South Africa leaving the Commonwealth (1961), British Guiana (1962-1964), Aden (1962-1967) and Rhodesia (1965-1979).

In this context Britain found it necessary to continue dismantling and freeing itself from its political Empire by granting independence to, inter alia, the Sudan (1955), the Gold Coast or Ghana (1957), Nigeria (1960), Somaliland (1960), Cyprus (1960), Sierra Leone (1961) Tanganyika (1961), Uganda (1962), Jamaica (1962), Trinidad (1962), Kenya (1963), Zanzibar (1963), Malaysia (1963), Nyasaland or Malawi (1964), Northern Rhodesia or Zambia (1964), Malta (1964), Singapore (1965), Barbados, (1966), Aden or South Yemen (1967) and Mauritius (1968). Notwithstanding this disengagement Britain of necessity became more economically and militarily dependent on the United States whose leadership of the 'West' was early recognized in the 'East' also by Australia and New Zealand as in the ANZUS Pact (1951) which ensured greater military collaboration with the United States, busy with Russian and Chinese containment in the Pacific area. The extension of America's role in the Middle East also became more marked under the Eisenhower Doctrine of the mid-fifties, after which Britain's presence there declined.

Over the next two decades the unwelcome realization began to dawn that not only had the roles of Britain as a great global and imperial power been dramatically reduced and support for the old fraternal

Atlantic or Anglo-American tie, the maternal connection with the white Commonwealth and the paternalistic connection with the black Commonwealth been weakened but, especially after the French 1961 and 1963 veto rebuffs about joining the EEC, and even after the luke-warm entry in 1973, her role as a leading European power was by no means assured. It was yet to be seen whether and in what form she would regain world stature or whether she would sink into a complacently affluent insularity and bathe, while the weather was still fair, in the familiar and congenial warmth of English-speaking culture.

One of Britain's ongoing problems was the failure of successive Conservative and Labour governments (using a variety of stop-gap Keynesian measures) to achieve for any length of time an effective management and control 'in the national interest' of her essentially capitalist economy located as it was in the wider, free-for-all and often cut-throat world capitalist system. A measure of growth and affluence was achieved, and was to continue unevenly throughout the century, but it did not mask Britain's continued economic divisiveness, imbalance, instability, nationalist insularity and relative productive decline.

There were still economists like Milton Friedman (Capitalism and Freedom 1962, etc) and P T Bauer (Dissent in Development 1971, etc) who believed in the universal beneficence at home and abroad of a free private enterprise economy with its allegedly invisible, anonymous, impersonal, automatic, responsible, competitive market mechanism. Other, more sociological social scientists, however, like J K Galbraith (American Capitalism: the concept of countervailing power 1952 and The Affluent Society 1958), M Harrington (The Other America: Poverty in the United States (1962), P Townsend in 1968-1969 studies later written up in Poverty in the United Kingdom, A G Frank (Capitalism and Underdevelopment in Latin America 1967, Latin America: Underdevelopment or revolution 1969) and G Myrdal (Asian Drama: An inquiry into the poverty of nations 1968 and The Challenge of World Poverty 1970) began to develop another view.

This was the revelation of the powerful controlling and often monopolist organizations dominating capitalist systems, the basic productive, exchange and distributional inequalities at their heart, the more advantaged and affluent participants and their sometimes irresponsible and unresponsive influence on others at home and overseas, the persistence of disadvantage and poverty both in developed and undeveloped countries, and the need to promote more generous social ideals and more vigorous 'political action' for a bottom-up democratization of economic systems throughout the world. However, notwithstanding her lengthy and considerable experience of and expertise in empire and commonwealth Britain now showed little enthusiasm or readiness to adopt that powerful and positive role in a capitalist-dominated Cold War world.

At the same time ideologically an increasingly self-concerned Britain was entering a more enquiring, affluent, hedonistic, permissive and later politically restive period. Advance in science continued, especially in chemistry (molecular biology, etc), medicine (physiology, computer technology, etc) and physics (electronic physics, radio astronomy, etc) with valuable popularizations like J Bronowski's The Common Sense of Science (1951) and J Huxley's Evolution as a Process (1954). In popular culture, against a sombre backdrop ideology of hawkish Cold War Anti-Communism together with a still richly colourful surround of British imperial values, several distinctive ideologies were to emerge. These included cynical or satirical literary 'movements', hedonistic youth and popular entertainment (now more widely disseminated through records, radio, television and press) and a range of radical or reformist political forms. These reflected sceptical reactions to the staid austerity of postwar reconstruction, the outmoded rigidities and constrictions of traditional society, the attempted superimposition of American, Russian and British Brave New Worlds, the survival of dangerously aggressive nationalism and imperialism, and the unresolved problems of racial, ethnic, linguistic, religious, sexist and class discrimination in so-called democratic society.

Examples are the 1950's literary cynicism, like that of K Amis (Lucky Jim 1954), P Larkin (Collected Poems, 1988) and J Osborne (Look Back In Anger 1956) all 'looking back' in their respective genially indifferent, drearily gloomy or angry anti-Establishment

style; the satirical fringe revues, media programmes and periodicals like Private Eye from the early 60's; the rebel, macho, Rock-and-Roll youth culture and Teddy Boy fashions of the 50's and the equally lively hedonistic and apolitical Pop culture of the 'Swinging Sixties' with Beatles and Rolling Stones pop and rock music, hippy-time Pink Floyd psychedelic music and drug-taking, Pop Art, bisexuality, the beachfront antics of Mods and Rockers, and the mod and mini-skirt fashions of Carnaby Street and the Kings Road; and the Protest or political folk music as of the early Bob Dylan.
A range of political movements included the Campaign for Colonial Freedom in the mid-1950's, the Campaign for Nuclear Disarmament (CND) and racist National Front movement in the late 50's and various left-wing Vietnam Solidarity and anti-American movements in the 60's, the SNP 'Put Scotland First' protest, the ethnic Welsh Language Society campaign and the more political and paramilitary Free Wales campaign against 'English' rule and second homes, the more violent extremist movements of Catholic republican and Protestant Unionist organizations like the Irish Republican Army (IRA) and the Ulster Defence Association and Ulster Volunteer Force in Northern Ireland, and the feminist movements (Germaine Greer, The Female Eunuch 1970, etc) in the 70's. These protesting organizations knew what they were against but they were less explicit or agreed about the Britain or Ireland or Wales or Scotland or England of the future they would like to see.

Britain retained a generally supported British monarchical, unitary government, centralized British economic and political institutions, a lengthy shared British history, and with English, a nationally and internationally recognized common primary language and much of a many-stranded British culture. There had long been and 'would always be' an England, Scotland, Wales, etc but Britain, long multicultural and now more multiracial remained the 'nation' in the sense of the largest effective community permeated by a sense of comprehensive solidarity. There was a sense in which it was now a less confident and cohesive nation. There was now something of a nostalgic fading of historic solidarity that had been based on economic and imperial power and the bulwark of close cultural ties with America and Commonwealth, and long embodied in a still partly surviving traditional institutional establishment. There were now strong secessionist or emerging devolutionary divisions as in Northern Ireland, Scotland and Wales, race relations and industrial problems in general, and a growing recognition of a need for institutional reform. Some politicians like Tony Benn believed that Britain could and would pull through by populist Workers' programmes, increased democratic participation and modernization. But despite the publication of several valuable studies of multi-racial, multi-ethnic and multi-religious plural societies, for example M Gordon's Assimilation in American Life (1964), M G Smith's The Plural Society in the British West Indies (1965), Smith and L Kuper's Pluralism in Africa (1969), R A Schermerhorn's Comparative Ethnic Relations (1970) and J Rex's Race Relations in Sociological Theory (1970) there was in this period little application of such sociological analysis to, or political debate about, British society and culture as a whole.

The third quarter of the twentieth century was the period also of the Korean War (1950-1953), the Festival of Britain (1951), the 1952 testing of the first American hydrogen bomb and the first British atomic bomb, the Coronation (1953), the Clean Air Act (1954) against London-like smog, the establishment of the UK Atomic Energy Authority (1954) the Geneva Convention (1954) proposing the settlement of the new nations of North and South Vietnam, Laos and Cambodia, the first British transmission of commercial television (1955), the final withdrawal of French colonial troops from Vietnam (1955), the War in Vietnam (1955-) with early American 'advisory' intervention and later increasing military involvement between 1965 and 1975, C P Snow's The Two Cultures (1956) advocating more attention to science, the invasion of Suez (1956), A Crosland's The Future of Socialism (1956), R Hoggart's The Uses of Literacy (1957) against commercialism, etc., the 1957 Soviet Sputnik launch and the subsequent Space Race, the testing of the first British hydrogen bomb (1957), the establishment of the European Economic Community (EEC) or Common Market (1957), the 1957 Council of Arab Economic Unity with later Arab Common Market and Arab Monetary Fund to promote economic development in Arab countries, and the Wolfenden Report (1957) with proposals about the permission of homosexuality. There followed R Williams' Culture and Society (1958), racial disturbances in Notting Hill, etc from 1958, the Local Government Act (1958), the Life Peerages Act (1958), the establishment of the Campaign for Nuclear Disarmament (CND) and the first Aldermaston March (1958), the testing of the first French atomic bomb (1960), the Local Employment Act (1960) giving incentives to private industrialists in depressed areas, R Crossman's Labour and the Affluent Society (1960), the first French veto of Britain's entry into the EEC (1961), the Cuban Crisis (1962), the Commonwealth Immigration Act (1962), A Sampson's The Anatomy of Britain (1962) and D Jay's Socialism in the New Society (1962), the 1964 introduction of the BBC 2 television service, the testing of the first Chinese atomic bomb (1964), the Housing Act (1964) and the establishment of the Welsh Office with a Secretary of State for Wales (1964).

It was also the period of the Race Relations Board and the Community Relations Commission, the Murder (Abolition of the Death Penalty) Act (1965), the 1966 to 1967 Sterling crisis and devaluation, after which many members of the 'Sterling Area' moved foreign exchange reserves out of sterling, and the 'area' gradually 'disappeared', the 1967 testing of the first Chinese hydrogen bomb, the Welsh Language Act (1967), the Abortion Act (1967) permitting abortion on certain grounds, the Sexual Offences Act (1967) legalizing homosexual practices in private between consenting adults, the second French veto of Britain's entry into the EEC (1967), Civil Rights disturbances in Northern Ireland (from 1967), the 1968 testing of the first French hydrogen bomb (1968), racial disturbances (1968), the Race Relations Act (1968), and the Student or Campus disturbances (1968-). There followed D Jay's After the Common Market (1968), the 1969 establishment of ARPANET (Advanced Research Projects Administration, the American Cold War military computer network, ancestor of the 1982 commercial INTERNET), the Downing Street Declaration (1969) to speed up the civil rights process in Northern Ireland, the establishment there of the Social Democratic Labour Party (1970), the operation of the Open University (1970), the Industrial Relations

Act (1971) to curb unofficial strikes, and the Commonwealth Immigration Act (1971).

Subsequent landmarks included the Coal Strike (1972), the Bloody Sunday disturbances in Northern Ireland (1972), the suspension of the Northern Ireland government in 1972, Britain's and Eire's entry into the EEC (1973), the ARPANET computer system extension to Britain (University College London, etc) in 1973, the Arab-Israeli war and OPEC oil crisis (1973), the establishment of the left-wing Campaign for Labour Party Democracy (1973), several Acts between 1973 and 1975 to improve the status of women, namely the Domestic Violence Act, Domestic and Matrimonial Proceedings Act, Guardianship of Children Act and the Sexual Discrimination Act, the Kilbrandon Report (1973) with its models of possible Scottish and Welsh devolution, to be followed by White Papers Our Changing Democracy: Devolution in Scotland and Wales (1975) and Devolution: the English Dimension (1976), A Crosland's Socialism Now (1974), and the Turkish invasion of Cyprus (1974).

In the final quarter of the twentieth century Britain was governed by Wilson's (and from 1976 Callaghan's) Labour ministry (1974-1979), Thatcher's first Conservative ministry (1979-1983) Thatcher's second ministry (1983-1987), Thatcher's third (and from 1990 Major's) ministry (1987-1992), Major's second ministry (1992-1997) and Blair's Labour ministry (from 1997).

This was the period, in the wider context, of the brief Cold War Detente in the 70's affecting in Britain the Labour ministries of Wilson and Callaghan followed, firstly by the resumed Cold War Confrontation of the 80's, matched in Britain by Thatcher's hawkish Conservative regimes, and secondly by the post-Cold War Coexistence of the 90's marked by American-led dominance of an aggressive global capitalist system, forming the back-drop of the Major and Blair administrations.

The high-point of the European Detente period was the SALT I Soviet-American arms control Agreement of 1972 following such earlier developments as the Sino-Soviet split, the 1968 US-Soviet Nuclear Non-proliferation Agreement (against German rearmament), the run-down of the Vietnam war, the Sino-American rapprochement and China's admittance to the UN, and the normalization of

German-Soviet relations (accepting two German states and a new status for Berlin). The Confrontation period, most emphasized in the early 80's by Reagan's massive military build-up and his 1983 Strategic Initiative Plan (SDI or Star Wars) to deploy weapons in outer space, included aggressive action to roll back communist influence both in the Third World (Nicaragua, Grenada, Afghanistan, Libya, Angola - with white South African cooperation - and Cambodia) as well as elsewhere as in Europe (Poland, etc) and in Taiwan in Asia. An easing of the confrontation began in the second half of the 80's, influenced by Gorbachev's initiatives in the interests of his internal glasnost (open government) and perestroika (economic restructuring) policies, and resulting in the Intermediate Nuclear Forces (INF) Treaty of 1987 and other agreements, and phased Soviet military withdrawals from Eastern Europe, (Berlin, East Germany, Poland, Hungary, Bulgaria, Romania, etc) and from the Chinese borders, Afghanistan and Cambodia in Asia, from Angola and Ethiopia in Africa, and from Latin America.

In the post-Cold War Coexistence period the USSR experiencing secessionist divisions and an internal drive for democratic political and liberal economic reform collapsed and was replaced by Yeltsin's Russian Federation. The decade was marked on the one side by the continued presence of the dominant American capitalist superpower, of several associated European and Asian capitalist great-powers, and of, across the world, a host of lesser, often undemocratic, capitalist nation states, and on the other side by the 'near' superpowers of an aspirant democratic and mixed-economy Russian Federation and a reforming but still communist Chinese People's Republic with a few lesser socialist nation state supporters like Cuba and North Korea. A Western scepticism and caution about communism and resistance to its re-emergence or development, notably in the poverty-stricken Third World, continued to and beyond the century's and millennium's close.

Even in the Detente of the 70's and despite indebtedness to the IMF international capitalist cartel Labour Britain continued to maintain its increasingly expensive independent nuclear posture and wary attitudes towards the EEC and towards Third World and Commonwealth initiatives. This was compounded by the right-wing

Conservative Cold War Confrontation in the 80's and 90's and close cooperation with America in defence policy, for example over the British siting of US Cruise missiles and related regional policies in Latin America and Southern Africa, in the 1986 bombing raids on Libya, in Middle East brokerage between the Arabs and Israel, and in the war in Kuwait in 1991.

On the world stage Thatcher like Reagan displayed a self-righteous , moralistic Crusader role against the threat of an 'evil' Communism. In trade she aggressively promoted British capitalist interests and economic nationalism. In the wider context she appeared unsympathetic to ideas of one-world or Commonwealth or European unity, to internationalist institutions like the United Nations, to black nationalisms, or to a major British lead and role in helping the undeveloped countries of the Third World. With the return of a Labour government in 1997 there were some prospects of less confrontational global and European foreign policies but these had not yet been realized at the end of the century.

Within Britain most of the last quarter was marked by radical, anti-collectivist, pro-business trends in economic policy (monetarism, privatization of industries and utilities, greater control of public spending, reduction of taxes, etc) and greater and more abrasive control of trade unions and public bodies (quangos, media, universities, schools, abolition of metropolitan authorities and curbing of local councils). However, notwithstanding the advantages gained by the increasing flows of North Sea oil and gas (from 1975) and a later world-wide expansion of trade (to 1987) bringing a welcome affluence especially to the wealthy and to young 'yuppy' professionals and new home-owning and shareholding-classes, a dogmatic belief in the beneficence of the market economy and rigid initial emphasis on monetarist strategy and on an associated mix of fiscal and exchange control policies failed to produce an 'automatic' stability of the economic system.

Compared with major European competitors it produced low economic growth, high unemployment, an increasingly unfair distribution, a high inflation rate, and the worst balance of payments. With a later Stock Market Crash (1987), substantial rise in unemployment (over 3 million for many years), recession and the run on the pound (1992) came a growing public disillusionment not-to-be-dispelled by a 1994-1996 recovery. The new Labour government (1997-) with suggestions of a return to a more cooperative and compassionate middle-of-the-road mixed capitalist economy and a more decentralized but still unitary British government appeared to be cast in a gently reformist Social Democratic rather than a Socialist and federalist mode. There was still confident political expression of a 'British nation' standing proud, if not yet 'in Europe', certainly secure in an Atlanticist 'international community' apparently primarily based on the familiar supports of Washington and London.

In this final quarter of the century there might be elderly memories of Britain's wartime national unity against the common enemy, the postwar 40's solidarity for national recovery and reconstruction, and the creation of a common collectivist industry and welfare state, and the subsequent Tory and Labour one-nation consensus of the 50's, 60's and early 70's in the management of an affluent mixed economy but many people had memories also of more recent disunity and instability. These included industrial unrest indicative of long-standing class divisions, and growing ethnic and racial tensions and violence stemming from the older multinational and newer multiracial composition of the British population. These had been only temporarily eased by the Downing Street Declaration (1969) committing the Northern Ireland government to speed up the granting of civil rights, the Sunningdale Agreement (1979) setting up a joint Catholic-Protestant executive, the Kilbrandon Commission Report (1973) on Scottish and Welsh Devolution, and the Race Relations and related Acts of 1965 and 1968.

As the final quarter of the century proceeded strikes were common especially in the first decade. Over most of the period there was frequent violence in Northern Ireland and at times also on the mainland. There were serious race riots or disturbances in London's Brixton, Liverpool's Toxteth and Manchester's Moss Side in 1981, followed by the Scarman investigation and Report (1982) which drew attention to an associated alienation stemming from unemployment, discrimination and police intolerance and insensitivity. Towards the end of the century there were signs of progress in these areas and the promise of new stabilities. Three 'Agreements' or Declarations in 1985, 1993 and 1998 pointed a way for Northern Ireland. Under the Hillsborough agreement British and Irish government leaders agreed that Northern Ireland would according to the region's majority wishes remain a part of the United Kingdom but that ministers would meet regularly to review the situation should those wishes change. In the Downing Street Declaration (1993) there was British government acknowledgement that it had no 'selfish or strategic interests in Northern Ireland' and Irish government acknowledgement that any change in the status of Northern Ireland would require the full consent of the regional majority. The Good Friday Agreement (1998) recorded all-party support for the election of an Ulster Assembly on the Scottish model, a North-South ministerial council for cross-border security, a British-Irish Council of the Isles to regulate 'national' relations, and an undertaking by the Irish government to remove any territorial claim to Northern Ireland from its constitution. In 1999 a new Northern Ireland Assembly was uneasily achieved.

Similar progress in Scotland and Wales came after Devolution Acts in 1978 and referendums in 1979 which revealed 51.6 per cent support for devolution by Scottish voters and about 25 per cent in Wales, with neither operation reaching the required 40 per cent total electorate support. Almost twenty years later in 1997 further referendums revealed a passionate Scottish swing to a two-thirds positive vote and a larger but still less enthusiastic Welsh swing to a 50.3 per cent positive vote on a low poll. These developments were to pave the way for the establishment of a Scottish parliament with tax-raising powers and a Welsh assembly with mainly deliberative functions which were formally opened in 1999.

Ideologically Britain continued to make scientific advance notably in biology, astrophysics and information technology. Richard Dawkins in the Darwinist tradition wrote best-sellers which spanned the period from The Selfish Gene (1976) to The Blind Watchmaker (1986). With his enthusiasm for exploration of 'the wonders of the world' and his ongoing interest in the origins of consciousness and in the use of information technology he seemed an excellent choice for the personal chair in The Public Understanding of Science at Oxford set up by Charles Simonyi of Microsoft. Theoretical physicist Stephen W Hawking produced a similar landmark layman's book, this time on astrophysics A Brief History of Time: From the Big Bang to Black Holes in 1988.

In popular ideology Britain although still with high unemployment and very blatant homelessness now stood squarely in a self-centred and complacent hedonistic age with a commercialized mass culture facilitated by the wider use of radio, press, paperback books, television and, as a new development, the computer net's World Wide Web. In popular culture, not only in the rocking realms of the punk and electronic pop of teenybop, late teen and twenties 'youth' but also in the more adult and more considered sedentary or horizontal realms of English literature, it was a 'me-first' period. This was characterized by apolitical personal preoccupation, by personal quests, consciousness and gratifications especially in group and domestic situations, by social cynicism, unease, revulsion and despair, and a ready sensory embrace of, or absorption in, rave-up and pop-concert psychedelic experience or, set in a disorderly psychic literary landscape, the morbid, macabre and grotesque fantasies of the magico-religious.

On the fringe there were political ideologies. Among these, not directly part of political parties, were those connected with the feminist and gay movements, and ecological organizations pressing for conservation and environmental protection. An important campaign was that of CND and feminist and other women supporters of unilateral nuclear disarmament who protested at Greenham Common in Berkshire where Cruise missiles were to be based.
The fourth quarter of the twentieth century was the period also of the positive 1975 Referendum on remaining in the EEC, the first deliveries of North Sea oil (1975), the 1975/78 Diamond Report on the Distribution of Income and Wealth in Britain, pointing to achievement of a 'substantial' redistribution towards equality', the Northern Ireland Peace movement (1976), the IMF crisis (1976/77), the Winter of Discontent (1978/79), M Gordon's Human Nature,

Class and Ethnicity (1978), Saddam Hussein's coming to power in Iraq (1979), the USSR invasion of Afghanistan (1979), seizure of the US Embassy in Iran (1979), and the US recognition of communist China (1979).

In the 80's there were the Iraq/Iran Gulf War (1980-1988) with Iraqi use of chemical weapons, the Housing Act (1980) permitting the sale of council houses, monetarist M and R Friedman's Free to Choose (1980), the Trade Union Act (1980), Independence of Zimbabwe (1980), Polish martial law (1981), P L van den Berghe's The Ethnic Phenomenon (1981), P T Bauer's acidic Equality, the Third World and Economic Delusion (1981), the Falklands War (1982), the US invasion of Grenada (1983) the Coal strike (1984/85), neo-conservative G Gilder's The Spirit of Enterprise (1984), the privatization of British Telecommunications (1984), M Harrington's The New American Poverty (1984), the USSR testing of a cruise type missile (1984), the bombing of Brighton's Grand Hotel (1984) and Martin Amis' cynical, hedonistic and materialistic Money: A Suicide Note (1984).

There followed the Church of England's Faith in the City Report (1985) with criticisms of the Conservative government's philosophy, Gorbachev's assumption of power (1985), the football riot in Brussels (1985), the Chernobyl nuclear accident (1986), monetarist A Walter's Britain's Economic Renaissance (1986), the bombing raid on Libya (1986), the Local Government Act (1986) abolishing the metropolitan authorities, the privatization of British Aerospace, Britoil and British Gas (1986) D Howell's Blind Victory (1986) against government economic policy, R Hattersley's Choose Freedom (1987), the Education Act (1988), the Charter 88 movement for a Bill of Rights (1988), D Marquand's The Unprincipled Society (1988), the establishment of the dissident writers' and intellectuals' journal Samizdat (1989), E Hobsbawn's Politics for a Radical Left (1989), the Tiananmen Square disturbance in China (1989), the Iranian death sentence declaration on Salman Rushdie (1989) and the USSR withdrawal from Afghanistan in 1989.

With the 90's came the freeing of Nelson Mandela (1990), Iraq's
occupation of Kuwait and the 1991 Gulf War with America and
Britain, the dissolution of the USSR and the dissolution of
Yugoslavia (both in 1991), the Queen's annus horribilis (1992),
Black Wednesday and the devaluation of the pound (1992) the
Council Tax replacement of the unpopular 1990 community charge
or Poll Tax (1993), the establishment of the Czech and Slovak
republics (1993), Yeltsin dismissal of the Russian Parliament (1993),
the US bombing of Iraq (1995) about refusal to allow inspection of
sites, W Hutton's The State We're in (1995) in favour of citizen and
republican solidarity, the Israeli-Palestinian Agreement (1995), the
bombing of Canary Wharf (1996), David Marquand's The New
Reckoning (1997) about decentralizing Britain in a Federal Europe,
the agreed surrender of Hong Kong to China (1997), the Australian
negative vote against a Republic (1999), the House of Lords Act
(1999) abolishing most hereditary peers, and Scottish, Welsh and
Northern Irish devolution (1999) which brings us back to the
regions, and Montgomeryshire and the environs of Gregynog.

INDIVIDUAL, SOCIETY AND SYMBOLISM

All this may seem a long way from Gregynog's quiet valley and the
lives of its people over the last five to six centuries. However, the
reality, I suggest, was just that. While of course part of their
domestic and traditional society and culture was local and regional,
the overall societal and cultural context, as all the Gregynog owners
in their different ways well knew, was already extensive with most
of its governmental, political, economic and technological, scientific,
literary and artistic, educational and media, and religious
organizations and their associated sub-cultures centred and generated
elsewhere, notably in Britain but also partially in Western Europe
and North America. Among these wider cultures of institutional
arrangements and ideological systems were democratic, capitalist,
socialist, scientific, western artistic, philosophical, Christian and
secular schemes.

Using such an approach we are challenged to consider such
questions as firstly, the real or existential relationship of the

individual to his society, culture and country and secondly, how these 'relationships' affect his conception of his individual self and social identity.

In the smallest, simplest societies, the individual's linkage with society is mainly of a basic, family-kinship-local community kind because there is no superstructure of governmental and other central organizations. Most of their inhabitants have a similar societal position and associated simple conformist culture. In larger, more complex, differentiated and stratified societies, even if the population is still homogeneous, individual societal positions and individual cultures in accordance with a choice of different social attachments and linkages and a choice of different cultural usages may vary and be less conformist.

Most complex, modern national societies are further complicated by being, like Britain, plural societies that is multi-racial and multi-ethnic societies including different ethnic sub-societies of ethnic groups, organizations and local communities or 'regional' homelands, and different ethnic sub-cultures of institutions (like distinctive language or other customs) and ideologies (like distinctive religions). Individual members of a plural society therefore may be linked to their national society and culture (like the British) in a yet more varied and non-conformist, and additionally ethnic, way and these linkages may affect, but not completely determine, their especially adult sense of identity.

The new members of a plural society come at birth with the physical imprint of heredity, the racial marks, of ancient European, Asian or African peoples whose distant tribes, nations, homelands, languages and cultures remain unknown and unnameable in the mists of pre-historical time. Thereafter in their early upbringing they receive the socio-cultural stamp of their parents, the social and cultural marks of more recent and better known historical peoples, Welsh or English, Scottish, Irish, Pakistani, Nigerian, Jamaican, etc (with their own traditional, now ethnic, cultures and homelands) who have become members of the same British nation-state with its nation-wide society, culture and country. In their later upbringing and/or adulthood (when as freer and more rational beings they have a measure of choice) they may adopt something of this wider national and international culture.

In such a plural society an individual's sense and conception of his identity may come to have not only misty ancient racial, together with still very old but more concrete ethnic, cultural dimensions but also a growing more 'modern' national and global orientation. The marks of race and the early stamp of ethnicity may be inescapable components of identity but these may be overlaid by, and lose some of their significance to, wider associations, attachments and allegiances. To an extent man, who is not a simple, carbon-copy societal product or a wholly determined and unquestioning cultural clone, is at centre a particular and interactive individual being who can, with rationality and courage, resist emotional and mystical engulfments and shape and guard his own more sound and 'true' identity.

In an earlier section when dealing with how the grounds of Gregynog might be improved, I recommended, inter alia, that a path be constructed to the summit of Warren Hill, a generous bench be installed for a view of the Hall, and a flag-pole be restored beside it on which, I light-heartedly suggested, the Red Dragon might be raised and seen to fly. On second thoughts (but I write as one not born in Wales or Britain or Europe) it may be that the time for national flags (Welsh, British or European) is over and we must now recognise a wider allegiance and mark it with an apter symbolism. With the continuation of an increasingly less ethnic and insular University of Wales context this may soon become more speedily obvious, accepted and assured.

FOOTNOTES

(i)   Thomas Parry, Chap 10. 'The Bequest to the University' in Glyn Tegai Hughes et al. Gregynog University of Wales Press, 1977, p.127.

(ii)   Richard Haslam, Powys, in The Buildings of Wales series, Penguin Books, University of Wales, 1979, p.202.

(iii)   Miscellaneous service buildings along the rear Service or Garden Road from near the Kitchen-and-Service wing onwards past the Office-and-Courtyard block along the Back Drive towards the Back Gate and the Tregynon road were kindly identified by Mr Jim Thomas in 1999. These were named as the Boiler House, Gardeners' Hut, part of a Kennels now a Forestry Shed, Estate Stables, a new Store Shed, a Paint Store, a Carpenter's Workshop now a Tool Store, a sometime Engine House and a Barn.

(iv)   Care should be taken in accepting the captioning of two photographs as Gregynog Hall, near Newtown, c.1880 and Gregynog Hall, c.1880 on page 114 of Eva Bredsdorff's compilation in the Archive Photographs Series Montgomeryshire (Chalford) 1996.
Eva Bredsdorff, Senior Museum Curator at the Powysland museum in Welshpool, reported in 1999 that the photographs according to the Museum's accession register were dated circa 1863 and were part of a set of stereoscopic photographs made by Robert Owen, 'bookseller, stationer, printer and bookbinder', Broad Street, Welshpool. She additionally recorded that the identity of the hall shown was 'uncertain' and the reliability of the Gregynog captions 'uncertain, could be Marrington Hall' [in Chirbury].
For these reasons I have not reproduced the photographs in this volume.

(v)   A brief 1999 visit to the cellars with Dr Chris J Arnold, then of the Department of Continuing Education at Aberystwyth University College, revealed a mixture of cellar bricks including in some sections earlier 21 x 6 hand-made and later 23 x 8 regular moulded bricks. These will need closer examination.

(vi)   See Haslam, op cit. pp 201-204. I am grateful also for
suggestions made by Dr T M Humphreys in 1999 communications.
See also footnote reference (viii).

(vii)   The Moses Griffith water colour which he captioned
Gregynog House, Mr Blayney's, Montgomeryshire was captioned
Watercolour by Moses Griffith, c.1750 in a University of Wales
Gregynog pamphlet (1988). In view of the painter's life-dates
(b.1749 d. 1819) this date is probably nearer 1775 or later. A
photograph of the drawing was hanging in recent years in the
Newtown Textile Museum.

(viii)   Among valuable sources listed by Dr T M Humphreys of
Llansantffraid ym Mechain are: R Haslam's 'A Note on the
Architecture of Vaynor Park', Mont. Collect. 65 (1977); Bodynfoel
(a farmhouse in Llanfechian) as pictured in Mont. Collect. Vol.5;
John Ingleby's water colour of Llandrinio Hall (S.E. of Four
Crosses) and a plan of Trefnant (Welshpool above Powys Castle)
both at the National Library; further references to Llandrinio Hall in
Mont. Collect. 28 p.250, 32 p.231, 61 p.78; Peter Smith, Houses of
the Welsh Countryside, and on Groombridge Place, Kent Oliver Hill
and John Cornford, English Country Houses CAROLINE 1625-
1685, Country Life Ltd, London, 1966.
I am also grateful to Mr W Corbett-Winder for permission to view,
and for other information about, Vaynor Park in 1999.

(ix)   For Groombridge see Hill and Cornford (op cit) pp 123-130

(x)   Future visitors to the field may be interested to search for
the site of a Medieval or Post Medieval 3-metre-wide
'Portman's ridge and furrow' (PRN 4747) so'arbitrarily' named by a
Clwyd-Powys Archaeological Trust field-worker on a site visit in
1978. It apparently lies somewhere in or near the area between the
assumed Griffith viewing position (X in Illustration XXIII) and the
present Director's house. The whole field was no doubt ploughed in
this fashion in early times before the overlay of varied agricultural
and construction activities of recent centuries.

(xi)   See W Scott Owen, 'Parochial History of Tregynon', <u>Mont.</u>
<u>Collect.</u> xxx, 1896.

(xii)   See Charles Rollo in Glyn Tegai Hughes et al, <u>Gregynog</u>.
University of Wales Press, 1977, pp 88-94.

BIBLIOGRAPHY

Bredsdorff, Eva, (compiler) Montgomeryshire in Archive photographs series (Chalford), 1996.

Ellis, E L TJ: A Life of Dr Thomas Jones CH, University of Wales Press, 1992.

Haslam R, Powys in the Buildings of Wales series, Penguin Books, University of Wales Press, 1979.

Hill, Oliver and Cornford, John, English Country Houses CAROLINE 1625-1685. Country Life Ltd. London, 1966.

Hughes, G T, Prys Morgan and J Gareth Thomas (eds), Gregynog University of Wales Press, 1977 including chapters on the Regional Setting (H Carter), the name Gregynog (Ifor Williams and Melville Richards), the Blayney period (P Morgan), the Estate and its Owners 1795-1920 (D Howell), Life at Gregynog between the Wars (P Morgan), Music during the Davies period (J Hywel), the Davies Art Collection (Rollo Charles), the Gregynog Press (Dorothy A Harrop), the Park and the Gardens (B S O Fox), the Bequest to the University (T Parry) and the University at Gregynog (G T Hughes).

Hughes, G T Unpublished Papers, 'Gregynog: History of the Hall' (1996); 'The Blayney Family' (May 1998); and 'Tregynon' (1998) (Copies provided by author).

Hughes, T W 'Gregynog: its History and Associations', The Montgomeryshire Society Year Book 1935-6.

Ingamells, John, The Davies Collection of French Art, National Museum of Wales, 1967

Jenkins, David (ed), The Historical Atlas of Montgomeryshire, Powysland Club, 1999

Land Agents 'Particulars of the Gregynog Estate, 1894 For Sale by Private Contract, Debenham, Tewson, Farmer and Bridgewater, Land Agents, London.

Greg-y-nog Estate, Newtown, Montgomeryshire For Sale by Auction, 28, 29, 30 and 31 October 1913, at the Town Hall, Newtown, Millar, Son and Co, London. (both of these kept in the Warden's Safe at Gregynog).

Owen, W Scott, The History of Gregynog typescript 1888. In the possession of Lord Sudeley; copies at Gregynog and the National Library of Wales.

Owen, W Scott, 'Arthur Blayney and his Home, Gregynog Hall', Montgomeryshire Collections xxv (1891).

Owen, W Scott, 'Parochial History of Tregynon', Montgomeryshire Collections xxx (1896).

Sandford, George, 'The Blayneys and the Hanbury-Tracys, Lords Sudeley' Montgomeryshire Collections xviii (1885).

Smith, Peter, Houses of the Welsh Countryside.

Sudeley, Lord, 'Gregynog before the year 1900', Montgomeryshire Collections lxii, 2(1971, issued June 1973).

Sudeley Lord, 'Toddington and the Tracys', Transactions of the Bristol and Gloucestershire Archaeological Society lxxxviii (1969)

White, Eirene, The Ladies of Gregynog, University of Wales Press, 1985.

INDEX OF PROPER NAMES

Hain, Peter 64
Hanbury-Tracy (see also Sudeley and Tracy)
Hardie, Keir 44, 45, 49, 60
Haslam, R 89, 90
Hawking, S W 84
Hayek, F 72
Hill, Oliver 90
Holland 38, 67
Hong Kong 86
Hughes, Cledwyn 62-64
Hughes, Glyn Tegai vii, 54, 57, 89
Humphreys, T M vii, 24, 28, 90
Huxley, A 71
Huxley, J 70, 75
Hyndman, H M 44

Independent Labour Party 49, 60
India 38, 40, 67, 70
Iran 85
Iraq 85, 86
Ireland (Eire) 40, 41, 44-46, 69, 71, 76-79, 82-84, 86, 87
Israel 67, 79, 81
Italy 40

Jamaica 73, 87
Japan 67, 71, 72
John, E T 61
Joicey, J 17-21, 49-50, 86-88
Jones, Brian iii, vii
Jones, Dora Herbert 51, 53, 55
Jones, Gerallt 57
Jones, Thomas (TJ) 51, 52, 54, 55

Kenya 73
Keynes, J M 71, 74
Kilbrandon (Crowther) Commission and Report 64, 79, 82
King Edward VII Welsh National Memorial Association 51, 52
Kipling, Rudyard 41

Korea 77, 80
Kuwait 81, 86

Labour Party (and Ministries) 45, 60-65, 68-74, 79-82
Labour Representation Committee 45, 60
Larkin, P 75
Latin America 68
Lawrence, D H 69
League of Nations 51, 52, 55
Lenin, V 66
Lewis, S 61
Liberals 49, 58, 59, 61, 62, 65, 68, 70
Libya 80, 81, 85
Llandrinio Hall (Four Crosses) 24
Lloyd-George, D 51, 61

Malaysia 73
Marquand, D 85, 86
Marrington Hall (Chirbury) 89
Marx, K 44
Maynard, R 55
Methodists 38, 47, 48, 58, 59
Middle East 68, 73, 81
Mill, J S 46
Morgan, Kevin 64, 65
Morris,W 44
Mulhearn, Tom vii, 57
Myrdal, G 72, 74

National Front 76
National Library of Wales 52
National Museum of Wales 52
NATO 73
Nesfield, W Eden 16, 17
Newtown 39, 41, 43, 90
New Zealand 40, 47, 71, 73
Nigeria 73, 87
Northern Rhodesia (Zambia) 73

INDEX OF SUBJECTS